W9-ACD-162

ALVAR AALTO   1
FURNITURE

First MIT Press edition, 1985
© Museum of Finnish Architecture
All rights reserved.

2 Editorial board:
Elissa Aalto
Juhani Pallasmaa
Tapio Periäinen
Aarno Ruusuvuori
Åke Tjeder

Editor:
Juhani Pallasmaa

Lay-out:
Juhani Pallasmaa, Juha Ilonen
(Igor Herler, his own illustrations)

Artek material compiled by:
Marja Pystynen
Ben af Schultén

Scale drawings of Artek models:
Martin Relander

Translation:
Michael Wynne-Ellis/Eeva Maija Viljo (Herler)
Martha Gaber Abrahamsen (Schildt)
Michael Wynne-Ellis (Parko, Aalto/Norri)
Stuart Wrede (Excerpts from Alvar Aalto's
articles. Courtesy of The MIT Press.)

Editorial secretary:
Eija Rauske

Typesetting:
Helsingin Dataladonta Oy Ab

Lithography:
Offset-Kopio

Binding:
Ilmari Reijonen Oy

Paper:
Iconorex, special matt 135 g

Type:
Helvetica light

Printers:
Frenckell, Espoo 1984

Library of Congress catalog card number: 84-62393
ISBN 0-262-13206-0

NK 2635 .F53 A233 1985

Alvar Aalto furniture

alvar aalto furniture

MUSEUM OF FINNISH ARCHITECTURE
FINNISH SOCIETY OF CRAFTS AND DESIGN
ARTEK

RITTER LIBRARY
BALDWIN-WALLACE COLLEGE

WITHDRAWN

The MIT Press
Cambridge, Massachusetts
London, England

4

Sketch of various furniture ideas from the 1940's.

As you know, you need a nail to make a soup. And to make furniture you need a basic element, a structural standard part, which modified in some way, appears in all pieces. Sine qua non: apart from its structural characteristics, the basic element must have a purposeful and style creating form.

My furniture is seldom, if ever, the result of professional design work. Almost without exception, I have done them as part of an architectonic wholeness, in the mixed society of public buildings, aristocratic residences and workers' cottages, as an accompaniment to architecture. It has been great fun designing furniture in this way.

In furniture design the basic problem from an historical — and practical — point of view is the connecting element between the vertical and horizontal pieces. I believe this is absolutely decisive in giving the style its character. And when joining with the horizontal level, the chair leg is the little sister of the architectonic column.

Actually, the only thing I have to show at this little exhibition is a new chair leg. That's the nail in the soup. All the rest are vegetables, very good but not absolutely necessary. It is, perhaps, a bit much to come again with a piece of bent wood, a chair leg, and that's why I feel so humble in front of my colleagues; a bit like Carl Larsson saying, "Sorry, but I've come with my old Karin."

Alvar Aalto's introduction to the catalogue of his exhibition at the NK department store in Stockholm in 1954

CONTENTS

PREFACE

Contemporary design is often criticized for its social exclusiveness and inability to harmonize with contexts beyond its own narrow aesthetic realm. The strained artistic ideals of our own time have failed to create a relaxed and comfortable atmosphere. Design today has made a sharp distinction between high culture and popular taste, concerning itself so much with novelty that it quickly loses its fashionable appeal.

Alvar Aalto's furniture designs are a superb example of the uncompromising spirit that has managed to overcome the barriers of style and taste, fashion and social class. Many of his creations — some approaching their first half-century — are in greater demand now than ever before. His pieces of furniture are at once modern and traditional, elegant and cosy. Though mass-produced they convey the pleasing imprint of handicraft and are equally at home in the domestic surroundings of everyday life as the magnificent buildings of cultural renown.

His designs are not the result of specific planning work. On the contrary, they evolved in connection with his architectural projects, deriving from his desire for a comprehensive design conceived as a total concept from the townscape down to the door knob. They developed from simple sketches through successive experiments and improvements to prototypes created in close collaboration between the architect and the craftsman. Consequently, only a few of the original sketches and production drawings remain and it is most difficult to date exactly the almost five dozen models manufactured.

It is believed that Alvar Aalto suddenly appeared in the forefront of the architectural avant-garde at the end of the 1920s through his convincingly mature and articulate designs in the International Style. Likewise, that he began his pioneering work as a furniture designer by immediately producing his bentwood masterpieces. Both these impressions are wrong. As both an architect and furniture designer he already had behind him an impressive decade of work and experimentation in the prevailing Nordic Classicist style. Until recently precious little was known about this phase, largely due to obliviousness of the classical roots of modernity, but also Aalto's own deprecation of the artistic merits of his early works.

The story of Alvar Aalto's furniture, from his first known work in 1919 to the latest bentwood variations by Artek, has been reconstructed here in four articles. Mr Igor Herler, architect and scholar, reveals the hitherto unknown designs of Aalto's youth; Mr Göran Schildt, Ph. D., author and Aalto's biographer, studies the evolution of his "trademark", the bentwood furniture, and the creation of the Artek company; Ms Marja-Liisa Parko, interior architect, formerly employed in the Artek Design Studio, recalls the relations between Aalto and the Artek Studio and touches on some of the technical aspects of production; and finally, Ms Elissa Aalto, Alvar's wife and partner, in collaboration with Ms Marja-Riitta Norri, writes on fixed furniture in Aalto's architecture as an organic extension of his designs for standard furniture.

This book does not purport to be a complete document of Aalto's furniture designs as numerous sketches and drawings, and photographs of prototypes which the master himself found unsatisfactory have not been included.

Juhani Pallasmaa

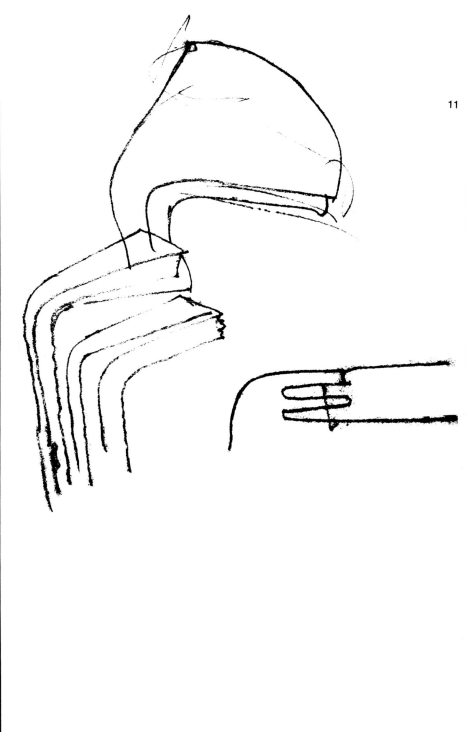

Sketch of the X leg, early fifties.

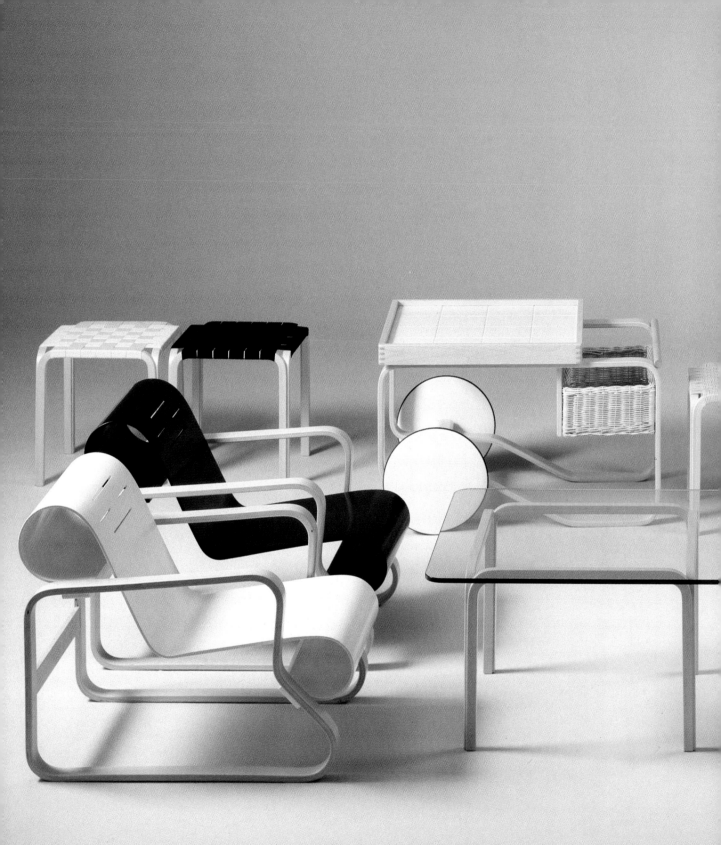

EARLY FURNITURE AND INTERIOR DESIGNS

IGOR HERLER

By the time the stackable three-legged stool came out in 1933[1], Alvar Aalto had behind him some fifteen years experience not only as an architect but also as a furniture designer. In other words, his stool designs, later to be regarded as classics in their genre, were by no means the first lucky shots of an amateur but works whose success was supported by experience gained over many years. This former image of him is widespread abroad and even in Finland, especially as Aalto himself gave indirect substance to the development of this myth. Namely, in his later years, he was apt to give out that his professional career actually only got under full steam in the last years of the 1920's, with Functionalism. As Functionalism believed itself to be the only correct form of truth, its supporters had to deny the achievements of their own youth, even, if these ran contrary to the tenets of the pure doctrine. Although Aalto, in his architecture, relinquished quite early on the use of the most canonized vocabulary of this style, he still seems to have adhered all the more faithfully to the conviction of those times that all past styles were of no interest and of little value. Thus it was neither essential nor even desirable to know anything about his earlier years, opinions, and works. Although it is not necessary to know about these disregarded years for a spontaneous evaluation in loco of Aalto's later buildings or furniture — though for a deeper understanding quite invaluable — for a full profile of the man himself this knowledge becomes absolutely essential.

What was this forgotten youth like? Just as colourful and eventful as one could wish, truly a biographer's treasure trove. Part of this glittering youth was tied to the unique conditions in Finland during its struggle to break away from the Russian Empire and gain independence; another part can be explained by Alvar's[*] own character, his "daredevil psyche": impulsiveness, enthusiasm, desire to experiment, and an unlimited faith in one's own abilities. In addition to studying and professional practice, this youth thus encompassed, on the one hand, his *"commitment for trial for Activist work in support of the Jaeger Movement",* and participation on the White side in the Civil War of 1918[2], and, on the other hand, a promising start to a career as a cartoonist, causerie writer, and art critic[3], and even a try at being a salesman for a gravestone works[4]. To this same youth also belonged such professional honorary positions as secretary to SAFA (the Association of Finnish Architects)[5], member of the board of Ornamo (the Finnish Association of Decorative Artists)[6], and building surveyor appointed by the Jyväskylä Town Magistrates' Office — whereby he even came to inspect some of his own elevations![7] These years further included Alvar's role as a popular educationalist and "performing" architect, the highlight being his broadcast commemorative talk on *"Man's attitudes towards aesthetic values"* given in Jyväskylä in 1925[8] and his most prolific period as a writer of articles and as interviewee (it was rumoured that he always wrote the interviews, too, himself)[9]. Some kind of terminal point to this fabulous youth was his heroic effort to gain the Professorship of Architecture at the University of Technology in a contest with J. S. Sirén who was then at the peak of his career. Although Alvar was found by 20 votes to 3 to lack the required competence[10], he nevertheless gleaned the following encouraging rhetoric from the experts: *"He is, undoubtedly, extremely talented and possesses considerable artistic potential which may in all probability in the future (...) come to leave a beautiful impression on our architecture."*[11]

•

Although a fair amount is known nowadays about the external events of Alvar Aalto's youth, precious little is known of his likings for and opinions on contemporary architecture and applied arts. Of Finnish architects at that time Alvar, together with Gustaf Strengell, did wield the most fluent pen, yet one seldom comes across any concrete declarations of programs in his writings until his Functionalist awakening, after which his statements were all the more self-confident. However, one can generally conclude that he in no significant way departed from the views of his generation, though perhaps he was fractionally more susceptible to new ideas as a result of his extrovert nature.

The attitude of the young to the ideals of the preceding period was, as usual, barren and cliché ridden; thus Alvar denounced, for example, the Finnish Jugend as *"that absurd 1905-period of the flowering of the birch-bark culture when all that was clumsy and coarse was considered so very Finnish".*[12] Apparently, too, he had as little respect for the great men of the Finnish Jugend, because

---

[*] When one has long studied the youth of another, though deceased person, one becomes so familiar with the subject that calling him by first name is almost automatic. So from now on the intimate Alvar will be used — and actually this only continues the practice among his professional colleagues already in his lifetime.

1

Alvar Aalto,
teollisuusnäyttelyn arkkitehti.

1

Alvar Aalto, a public figure at 24; newspaper illustration from 1922, in connection with the Tampere Industrial Exhibition.

he called his little daughter's kitten after Eliel Saarinen. [13] Despite their natural antagonism, here in Finland these two generations had also a number of features in common. Behind their assumed shield of nationalism both systematically used international stylistic forms (due to the superficiality of Finnish research, this basic characteristic has until now remained unemphasized in respect to the Jugend period). The young Alvar saw in this an indication of strength, not weakness: *"When we see how past ages have been able to be international and unprejudiced yet have remained faithful to themselves, we can with open eyes accept the influences of ancient Italy, Spain, and the new America."* [14] Yet, all countries were not equally acceptable as examples; Alvar might, for instance, remark that, *"the Paris of today is useless to us as a teacher in the applied arts".* [15] However, more surprising, considering the current orientation of Finnish politics, is his negative attitude towards Germanism in all fields of art. Exactly how this corrupting trend manifested itself remains somewhat unclear, but it was, in his opinion, at least widespread, for *"German advertising art and exhibition aesthetics seem to run instinctively in our blood"* [16] and it appeared *"that sometimes even the critics retain a substantial dose of German art notions".* [17] This *"spiritually suffocating life based on the German instinct for organization which, in our country for instance, lies like a thick crust preventing the appearance of natural architecture suited to the cultural development in a dignified manner"* [18] produced in Alvar's writings an opposite polarization, first towards Scandinavianism and a few years later to Latin culture. The former was *"nearer both spiritually and geographically"* [19], the latter's advantages being, for instance, *"intellectual flexibility"* and *"the spontaneous joy of creation",* as a result of which *"the external appearance of even the most modest of dwellings had been created in the boundless joy of a sudden impulse deriving from the immediate and natural comprehension of beauty".* [20]

In fact, Alvar's student period happened to coincide with that transition phase where a new, playful and daintily graceful trend, "Light Classicism" as I term it, penetrated into Nordic architecture and applied arts as one alternative to the earlier prevailing taste for monumental gravity. What specifically characterized it was its aim at momentariness, spontaneousness, thus even an architect's drawing was changed into something deliberately sketchy. This last flowering form of Classicism became the style particularly of the younger generation; its successful mastery required, namely, a spiritual flexibility and a certain ironic distance from the great stylistic inheritance, an over-reverential attitude was not beneficial. The main stars of this trend in

Sweden, E. G. Asplund and Sigurd Lewerentz, had not for nothing belonged to just that group of students of the Academy of Art who had founded their own school in 1910, having become fed up with precisely the excessive emphasis on the Antique and the Renaissance in academic teaching! [21]

•

What was it then that aroused Alvar Aalto's interest also in the arts and crafts — and specifically in furniture design? Actually, this is a futile question because at that time such fields were considered natural to architects. Whatever personal opinions Alvar may have held of Finnish Jugend and its leading exponents, the professional extensiveness launched at the turn of the century still served as the unofficial norm for the architects' field of activity. The example of Sweden had also a similar influence because there the role of young architects in the development of their country's applied arts was particularly prominent. A readiness to design bedroom or diningroom furniture for families of one's acquaintance, or chairs, tables, and coat racks for the public buildings they were planning was thus a normal part of professional routine in those days. However, no more than a superficial knowledge of production techniques was then required; so long as ordinary forms were adhered to, a craftsman could take care of the constructional problems. Finnish architects did not, in fact, go beyond the designing of unique pieces of furniture; creating models for large-scale production was not yet, for some reason, practised by the profession. Still, they were not averse to designing models for industry: for example, in 1912 from the more than a hundred types of Dutch-tile stove designs in production at the Helsinki factory of Wilh. Andsten, two-thirds were attributed to architects. [22]

In those years people in the applied arts in Sweden launched the *"vackrare vardagsvara"* (More Beautiful Things for Everyday Use) movement: its goal being to gradually steer craftsarts in a more industrial direction, the expensive but high-quality individual product was to be replaced by a cheap though still high-quality mass product in order to create a uniform and democratic taste. Despite exhibitions, propaganda booklets and advisory councils on taste, practical achievements remained meagre, and at the International Exhibition of Decorative and Industrial Art in Paris in 1925, Sweden again appeared more as the representantive of exclusive rather than social production. The rhythmic slogan was readily quoted also in Finland, but usually while at the same time deploring the lack of support in this country for the ideal. [23]

In the 1920's in Finland most furniture was at least nominally industrially manufactured, although in reality made to such a degree by hand and in such small series that they hardly differed from the singly turned out traditional craft products. In practice the Finnish furniture industry was divided into two lines; most of the manufactories concentrated on suites and ensembles and only a few on the making of individual pieces. In addition, there were some metal-working companies assembling iron bedsteads and firms which had specialized in American-style oak office furniture. The "better-class" sets of furniture made by the largest manufactories, as well as the intricately worked luxury items that were the focus of interest at fairs and exhibitions, were already, in general, the work of furniture designers trained at the Central School of Applied Arts. On the other hand, the cheaper domestic products on sale were almost without exception still turned out by craftsmen themselves on the basis of more or less international models.

•

The roots of Finnish applied arts of the 1920's and thus also of furniture design, clearly lie in the preceding decade; in actual fact, the beginnings of the period's style should be placed in the First World War. That was the time when the new Scandinavian Classicistic wave began to reach Finland, and the late-Jugend that had until then linked Finland mainly to Germany and Austria began to give way. The war naturally overshadowed everything, yet stylistic development progressed though concrete results in the form of furniture and objects were accountably fewer than under normal conditions. It is not, however, easy to obtain an overall picture of Finnish applied arts at that time: behind its Classicistic exterior the new period was anything but uniform in its concepts of form. It was marked by several parallel and overlapping endeavours, albeit from today's perspective these may look much the same in their ultimate result. In analyzing this finely divided multiplicity of ideas it is perhaps necessary to try to specify and characterize the most important trends that differ clearly from each other and at the same time to create a background on which to position Alvar Aalto's work of the twenties.

One of the components was still Jugend, though not in the form favoured by the uncouth taste of the first years of this century, but the cultivated and urbanized later version just mentioned; even this should have belonged to the past, at least in the opinion of the active designers. In reality, as late as 1924 the furniture design book issued by the Kansanvalistusseura (Society of Popular Education) was still offering as entirely up-to-date a fifteen year old set of pure Viennese Jugendstil furniture [24] and even in 1928, Lahden Puuseppätehdas Oy company was producing per year a couple of hundred sets of drawing room furniture that would have done honour even to Louis Sparre. [25] In itself this is not so astonishing; it is once again a case of that retardation in the habits of taste always prevailing between, on the one hand, the avantgarde and, on the other hand, the general public and manufacturers. Jugend influences were also to be seen in the furniture manufactured by two companies in Central Finland, Muuramen Tuolitehtaan Oy and Wilh. Schaumanin Vaneritehdas Oy. [26] From the point of view of the subject at hand, this production is of importance in so far as it composed one of the basic form worlds in Alvar's home town of Jyväskylä in both private homes and public buildings. Both factories had specialized in long series of individual items such as kitchen chairs and tables, wardrobes, bookcases, flower stands, clothes' racks, screens, rocking chairs, bedsteads, etc. In other words, typical pieces of complementary furniture which, in poorer circumstances, could be assembled to form practically all the furnishings in a home. Muurame's collection in particular was to a large extent based on Gebrüder Thonet factories' well-known Viennese furniture with its steambent wooden pole frames and plywood seats and backs.

But most furniture being offered then was representative of Classicism and its differend interpretations. The subdivision discussed in the following mainly illustrates the relationship of these interpretations to their origin, degrees of variance from stylistic orthodoxy and attitudes towards designing on the whole.

The easiest to recognize is the "Historicistic trend" that used old forms as such, unchanged. Thus, the object was not even the creation of something new on the basis of the old, but a kind of facsimile production; consequently at its purest it was copying of originals in museums. [27] Generally, though, it meant the making of slightly simplified variants of the popular Rococo, Gustavian, or Biedermeier sets of furniture; problems, however, cropped up when the original suite lacked a certain item, for instance, a bookcase.

It is a little more difficult to define the predominate line for

a

b

c

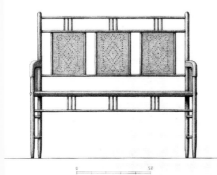

Finnish variations of Viennese bentwood furniture and even Late Jugend models were still popular.   a. Muuramen Tuolitehtaan Oy's sofa No. 32, 1:25.   b. Lahden Puuseppätehdas Oy's armchair No. 50.   c. W. von Essen's dressing table design from c. 1910 in a 1924 collection of models, 1:25.

2

a

b

Umklapptisch. 1790—1800

Bord, björk, polerad.
R. 2259. 55/40.

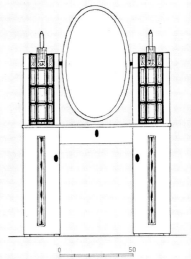

3

The "Historicistic trend" was content to copy earlier styles as such without any particular artistic objective.   a. American folding table from the late 18th century.   b. The Swedish David Blomberg Ab's "facsimile" from the 1920's.

a

b

4

"Normal Classicism" took its clues from the whole European upper class tradition whereas the "Folkloristic trend" only drew from vernacular versions of period furniture.   a. The Swede Carl Malmsten's design for a chair and serving cupboard from c. 1925, 1:25.   b. Oy Helylä's cupboard from 1927.

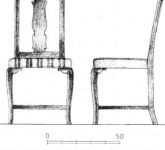

0   50

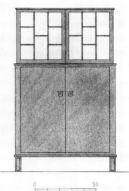

0   50

a

5   The simplicity characteristic of "Light Classicism" was often enlivened with some light jokes at the expense of the "sacred tenets of art".   a. Yrjö Lindegren's design for a cupboard from 1925, 1:30. b. The keyhole escutcheon for a funeral chapel from 1920 drawn by the Swede E. G. Asplund. c. Alvar Aalto's sketch of an "architectonic couple" from 1923, 1:80.   d. The Swede Uno Åhrén's "walking bureau" from 1923.

b c   d

Aino as an independent furniture designer : dining room suite   6
in oak with an "English" air, the main prize in the Finnish
Society of Crafts and Design's lottery in 1922; measurement
drawing 1:33.3.

0   1   2

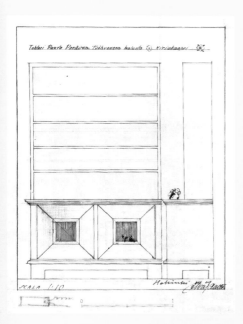

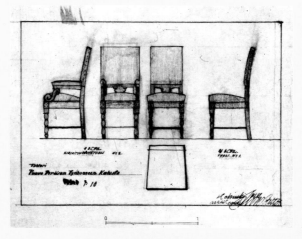

7 Alvar's first known furniture design reveals both the stylistic difficulties and graphical clumsiness of the novice. Drawings for study furniture from 1919, 1:40.

The differences in nature can be seen in both the handwriting and the signatures: Alvar is always in the limelight, Aino retiring into the background.   a. Signatures on a limited competition entry from 1926, 1:1.   The share of both in the project can be seen from the "box-stamps" on the working drawings.   b and c. Stamps filled in by Alvar, 1:2.5. d. Stamp filled in by Aino, 1:2.5.

8

b

c

d

a

the whole period, "Normal Classicism", the form seen most in the works of our leading furniture designers Arttu Brummer-Korvenkontio, Birger Hahl, Margaret T. Nordman, Harry Röneholm, and Werner West; its most full-fledged representative in the Northern Countries was the Swede Carl Malmsten. It differed from Historicism in respect to its overall creativeness: the earlier styles provided the starting-point for further development but by no means a ready-made and final solution. It was a matter of using models for inspiration, not of copying them. What typified this "Normal Classicism" was a certain solemnity and an almost desperate striving for "good taste". It was probably subconsciously feared that *"the worship of the unbridled, often uncontained imagination"* and *"artistic freedom"* [28] of the early Finnish Jugend would once again take power if a proper sense of responsibility was not maintained. The hope had probably been for a uniform and stable form culture in our own or in the Scandinavian spirit; in the period's own opinion, this was never achieved as there were too many stylistic attractions to choose from among the two and a half thousand year tradition of Classicism; predominant, however, were the trends from the Swedish-Finnish period from Baroque to the Gustavian Style. [29] Division was further increased by the inconsistency which was troubling the Finnish applied arts: whilst acknowledging the need for and importance of a *"vackrare vardagsvara"* industrial production, the world-famous Swedish luxury handicrafts were envied and copied. It was from the latter that the show-pieces of Finnish "Normal Classicism" furniture originated — decorated with Henry Ericsson's wood intarsias or Hannes Autere's wood carvings. The moderation and economy in form and materials demanded by the former trend, on the contrary, brought forth problems; when furniture that would serve the modest living standards of the middle class were purposely sought through competitions, the entries were often of a *"character more befitting a salon, boudoir or squire's room than a simple living room".* [30]

Somewhat similar to the above was the "Folkloristic trend" in which the basis was vernacular versions of period furniture, for in the wake of the renascent Classicism came an interest in peasant culture. Now at last the buildings, furniture, textiles, and objects of the farming areas of West Finland were exciting admiration. Finnish Jugend, which always prided itself on its nationalism, had never been able to suffer this kind of Finnish folk art because it showed genteel and Classicistic influences. The most conspicuous beneficiary of this form world was the Kotiteollisuusosake-yhtiö Pirtti company, founded in 1911, which marketed pieces of furniture made by rural artisans to the company's

designs. [31] Some of these were copies of traditional models, others more freely interpreted, yet still recognizable within the vernacular mould. Apart from decorative painting, a truly unpretentious effect was aimed at by using only a thin glazing of oil paint in the finishing.

Of all the trends based on Classicism, the most original and, artistically speaking, most creative was "Light Classicism" characterized as it was by the slightly ironic relationship to the forms inherited from antiquity as described earlier. These forms were intentionally used as mere tools in aiming at an overall effect and thus were no longer valued so much for their own sake, rather they tempted to a gently joking treatment. In architecture, for example, columns could be stretched and thinned without limit, so that in the end they looked more as if they were hanging limp from the entablature rather than supporting it. A continuous hovering on the borders of good taste and concealed jokes of a kind were also typical: the triangular nose aperture and eye socket of a skull might form the keyhole for the door of a funeral chapel or in a masculine row of pillars one might acquire a "wife", a feminine counterpart with rounded baluster shape. [32] Similar kinds of sophisticated features appeared in the applied arts, too; Classicistic themes were often mere hints and could make a disjointed impression, their significance to the context depending much on the beholder's own associations. When a young Swedish architect turned to the Empire Style for naturalistic lion's paws and placed them as supports under a chest of drawers of an otherwise totally abstract, almost crystalline appearance, this exaggerated "orthodoxy" was, of course, quite deliberate and understood by his friends but could leave the older generation of designers dumbfounded. [33] This extreme form of "Light Classicism" with intellectual emphasis appeared, however, relatively rarely in furniture and was actually applied by architects only. In its more conventional form this trend mainly resembled the simplest versions of the late Gustavian Style or early Biedermeier, yet despite this it retained its unique freedom from restraint that set it apart from "Normal Classicism".

Finally, it is worth touching briefly on the stylization and simplification of traditional themes in the Classicism of the 1920's as there exist frequent misunderstandings in regard to its character and origins. It is not a question of, for instance, a provincialism, an unintentional change in style due to geographical and cultural distance, because the deformation of forms was now entirely deliberate and practised for definite purposes. In this case, Scandinavian Classicism was not some distant reflection of a Continental phenomenon, as so many styles before had been, but an independent, even exportable trend, that was specifically created here. Neither is the simplification to be viewed as evidence of budding Functionalism, however tempting the idea appears. Rather the period's affection for smoothness, shallow mouldings, and sparse details is to be seen as normal to Classicism, as the other extreme in the continuous wavelike movement of its general comprehension of form; the previous similar, less expressive period, for instance, in architecture had been in the 1840's to 1860's.

In the above, the demarcations between the different trends have been deliberately exaggerated, whereas in practice they seldom appear so clearly, particularly when one and the same work may well combine many stylistic tendencies.

•

In commencing a closer examination of Alvar Aalto's furniture design in the 1920's there is good reason at the very beginning to consider the question that inevitably crops up sooner or later when evaluating Alvar's career: what was the role of his wife, Aino Marsio-Aalto, in those works that carry both their names? It is no longer possible to arrive at an unambiguous answer, at best one can draw some general conclusions. Too little is actually known about Aino, the main reason being, of course, her own retiring and even nature which made her fade into the background behind a husband who was always in the footlights. The usual interpretation of Aino's role has thus been slightly underrating; she is considered to have had little actual creative ability even though she was professionally competent. Her importance is seen more in that safe conventionalism that so naturally complemented and evened out the boundless idea production of her husband, or as the Swede Gregor Paulsson so poetically put it: *"Fire and calm waters had become one."* [34] This idyllic image is not necessarily quite true, for even in those few works of the 1920's and 1930's executed in Aino's own name and known to us, one is tempted to see too much independent talent to wholly accept the idea of her as a mere motherly Demeter type.

Aino was somewhat older than Alvar and had thus also qualified as an architect earlier; the subject of her diploma work was a kindergarten [35] (at one time she had thought of becoming a nursery-school teacher). [36] She must have become acquainted with interior design already during her student years as the first known work by her, a set of furniture designed for the first prize in the Finnish Society of Crafts and Design's lottery in 1922, would hardly have been

commissioned from a beginner. [37] Seen from today's perspective, this 8-person dining room suite in oak has been designed with a sure hand, yet it is, at the same time, a rather ordinary example of "Normal Classicism", characterized by its massiveness and lack of ornament. Its value actually lies precisely in its typicality because in it are reflected two objectives, seemingly contradictory but characteristic to the period: on the one hand, an aspiration towards bourgeois dignity and, on the other hand, in accordance with the Swedish recipe, a programmatic unobtrusiveness. The overall "Englishness" chosen fulfills, however, remarkably well both objectives ("Englishness" in this context being but an epithet descriptive of the established bourgeois domestic culture rather than a title for a particular style). The dining table is, in any case, Elizabethan in style — with cup-and-cover legs and extendible top — but considerably simplified. The stylistic origin of the small chairs alongside the table and those with arm rests at either end for the host and the hostess is more concealed, one could perhaps read into them a Chippendale influence, at least in respect to the straight legs of even thickness. The 18th century type low bracket feet with their decorative "ears" are sufficient to give to both the glass-fronted china cabinet and the wide sideboard the desired English effect; the commercial name for the latter type of furniture in Finland and Sweden was, in fact, often "sideboard" although in external appearance it is more reminiscent of the "credenza" of the Italian Renaissance than any English type. The small serving cupboard ultimately displays a glimpse of the jocular mood belonging to "Light Classicism" — because it can hardly be a question of ignorance — for the four keyholes on the front do not belong, as one would imagine, to four drawers but to a pair of doors behind which are the drawers for the cutlery. The whole suite is finished in dark brown; unfortunately, the chair's original reddish upholstery has been replaced.

It was mere chance that Alvar did not happen to write a newspaper critique of the work of his future wife; he was conscripted into the army in the summer of 1922 which severed just in time his career as an art and design critic. [38]

Alvar's first known furniture designs, on the other hand, date from 1919 and they were made for the dentist brother of a classmate from Jyväskylä. [39] His draft, consisting of a bookcase, sofa table, desk chair and four small chairs, is in its stylistic uncertainty touching enough to make one believe it to be his first effort in this field. One can also see the characteristic clumsiness in drawing which stayed with him all his life; he never became a master of architectural

a   b

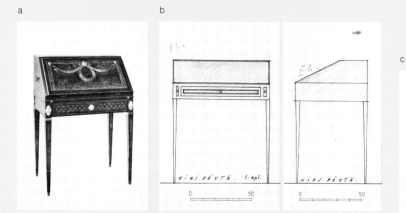

c

In a 18th century Gustavian Style secretaire especially the simple basic form appealed to furniture designers of the 1920's.   a. Secretaire made by the Swede Georg Haupt jr. (1741—84).   b and c. Design by Aino and Alvar; sketches 1:30 and illustration based on the working drawing.   9

a   b

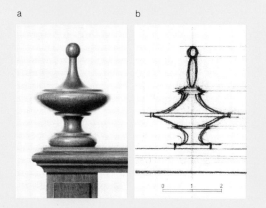

10

The stylistic tolerance of "Light Classicism".   a. The symbol of the despised 19th century Neo-Renaissance, the turned knob.   b. Detail of internal decoration of the secretaire designed by Aino and Alvar, 1:1,25.

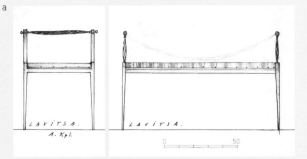

a

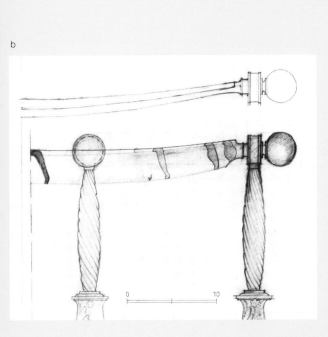

b

The genuineness of the materials was not of particular significance in the 1920's, the goal — form — was more important; originally the part hanging like a leather strap between the uprights of the arm rests was to have been carved from wood.   a and b. Design for tabouret by Aino and Alvar; sketches 1:25 and detail from working drawing 1:4.

11

Scandinavian sewing tables from the 1920's.   a. The Swede E. G. Asplund's model from 1920.   b. Werner West's model from 1921.   c and d. Design by Aino and Alvar; sketch 1:25 and illustration based on working drawing.

12

a b

c

d

a

b

13   The decorative theme running through the whole suite, the half or full sunburst motif, was in this form of American origin.   a and b. Design for wardrobe by Aino and Alvar; sketch 1:33.3 and as executed.

14

Sometimes it is possible to trace the source of the idea from a specific picture in a book or magazine.   a. American early 18th century highboy.   b and c. Design for linen chest of drawers by Aino and Alvar; sketch 1:33.3 and as executed.

a

b

c

15

The history of the tapering and recessed "side panelling" of the Seinäjoki Civil Guards' House pillars?   a. Leg of linen chest of drawers, 1:3.3.   b. Table leg from the early 1920's, 1:20.   c and d. Civil Guards' House pillar from 1925; sketch and as constructed, 1:75.

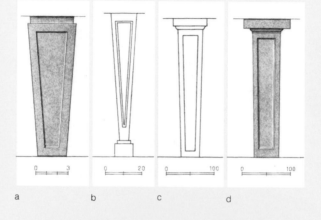

a   b   c   d

a

16   An original solution to the social aims of the applied arts in the 1920's : Royal furniture for all !   a. American early 19th century four-poster.   b and c. Design for bedstead by Aino and Alvar; sketch 1:40 and as executed.

b

c

a   b   c

It is possible to apply the same details to both furniture and buildings.   a and b. Decorative urn on bed post designed by Aino and Alvar; working drawing 1:5 and as turned.   c. Decorative finial on the canopy of the Jyväskylä Workers' Club from 1925.

An example of the connections between Scandinavian and English furniture design that have prevailed over the centuries.   a. A Chippendale-style tripod table from the 1750's, 1:25.   b and c. Design for bedside table by Aino and Alvar; sketch 1:20 and as executed.   18

a   b

c

a

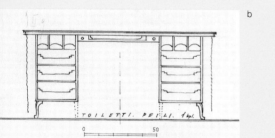

b

c

19

The transformation of the dressing table from a ceremonious "altar to beauty" into a conventional and practical writing desk.　a. First design by Aino and Alvar, illustration based on working drawing.　b and c. Second design; sketch 1:25 and as executed.

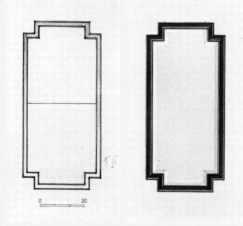

a

b

20

An anachronism of the Classicism of the 1920's : the mirror glass was intended to have been made in two parts as in the 18th century.　a and b. Design for mirror by Aino and Alvar ; sketch 1:25 and as executed.

graphics in the pure sense of the word but remained a passionate sketcher whose ideas others transcribed into a publishable form when required.

Very little is known of the other work on furniture done by Alvar during his student years; he did design a double bed and bedside tables for his brother Väinö and sister-in-law Toini upon their marriage in 1921. [40] In the previous year, along with other members of Ornamo, he designed some of the sections at the first Finnish Fair and these were even awarded diplomas, [41] but this was more in the line of decorators' work. Probably with this Fair in mind the *"Taideteollisuustoimisto Aalto & Ericsson"* was set up, too, the partner being Henry Ericsson who was later to become a well-known decorative painter and glass designer. [42] All the evidence would indicate that the company existed more on paper than in reality, but the motion still gives a good picture of both the youthful, far-reaching ambition and the precocious officialness that always coloured young Alvar's activities.

·

Alvar Aalto's actual career in furniture and interior design began in the early spring of 1924 when he was commissioned to design the interior of quite a large café and the bedroom furniture for a classmate. It is here that the problem of Aino's role, mentioned earlier, crops up for the first time. At this stage Aino and Alvar were not yet married, though in all probability already courting; officially Aino was thus only a bureau assistant. [43] Alvar had had a few "drudges" before that, among others, the decorative painter Valter Wahlroos [44], but Aino was the first one as qualified as himself and also accustomed to working on her own. [45] The only source from which one can try to assess their individual contributions are the drawings, but here, too, one must proceed on the unofficial assumption that Aino was taken on to help out in the pile of work that had accumulated in the bureau as an independent designer and not merely as a draughtswoman. The previous Christmas the bureau had taken into use a "box-stamp" for working drawings which had to be filled in with the number of the job and drawing, the date, and the drawer's initials. [46] The information revealed by these stamps is not, however, all that reliable because, at least in the beginning, Alvar appears to have stamped the drawings and filled in the data at a later date, naming himself as the drawer even though the work is clearly that of Aino. Even taking into consideration Alvar's boundless energy and capacity for generating

ideas, it is difficult, when studying the drawing material from that period, to come to any other conclusion than that Aino's share in the interior design work, particularly in these early years, must have been quite decisive.

The bedroom furniture ordered by the classmate can be evaluated on the basis of both the design and the execution. [47] Although not all the pieces planned were ever made, in other respects the local craftsman seems to have followed the drawings faithfully; the final result thus illustrates, more or less authentically, the tastes and competence of Aino and Alvar at that time.

The writing desk, which remained only on paper, was of the Gustavian secretaire type with drop-front and pull-out lopers so popular in the twenties; this model was also included, for instance, in the production of the David Blomberg Ab company in Sweden. [48] The original examples had been the secretaires made by the best-known Swedish 18th century cabinet maker, Georg Haupt, Jr. [49] Although the exaggerated slenderness of the legs (the cross-section of the lower end being only 1,4×1,4 cm) is in itself derived from the Gustavian Style, it also tells of the designers' still rather fumbling knowledge of materials. The same slight structural under-dimensioning is also to be seen in both the single and double tabourets, which likewise remained unexecuted; in its other parts, however, the latter was the most studied and detailed piece in the whole suite. The life-size working drawing included, for example, many small cross-sections of the arm rests to ensure that the craftsman's work would be in strict accord with the designer's wishes. The same arm rests contained an interesting contradiction between form and material: the curved piece hanging freely between the upright supports gives the impression of a leather strip, although it was intended to be carved of wood; these were, however, the typical gimmicks of "Light Classicism". The all-too serious *"vackrare vardags-vara"* movement for its part viewed these devices with misgiving and vehemently demanded honesty in the use of materials. [50]

The design for a sewing table, complete with cloth pouch suspended under the lid, was a combination of E. G. Asplund's well-known and already mass-produced model and its Finnish equivalent which had been designed by W. West. [51] Although the stack of drawers of the former table, diminishing like steps, had now been omitted, it was still to be seen in the suite: lifted on the top of the linen chest of drawers. In actual fact, there its origin was quite another, the model being a certain type of American 18th century highboy in which this unusual structure appears — the picture had been found in a book on Colonial furniture design.[52] The variant thought up by Aino and Alvar is, in its overall form, more balanced but undeniably also more ordinary; the disequilibrium between the original model's heavy, rectilinear upper part and long cabriole legs and butterfly-like handle plates has been, however, avoided in changing to short legs and Gustavian ring drop handles.[53] This American highboy provided ideas for other pieces, too: such as the semi-circular fan or sunburst ornament on the secretaire and the plain wardrobe.

The downward tapering and "panelled" sides of the legs on both the linen chest of drawers and wardrobe are Gustavian features[54]; in this connection the shape of the foot is perfectly appropriate, but Aino and Alvar carried through their "Light Classicistic" playfulness by using the same form in buildings, although ten times larger in size. The pillars supporting the ceiling of the auditorium of the Seinäjoki Civil Guard House are thus not of Cretan origin as has been claimed[55] but the reverse of a theme which Alvar later crystallized in the statement *"the chair leg is the little sister of the architectonic column".*[56] It belongs, of course, to the nature of Classicism that despite the difference in scale, the same details and in some cases even the same overall disposition can be applied to both buildings and furniture. Thus it is no surprise to find other familiar features of Alvar's architecture in the furniture designed for his schoolmate; the skillfully turned Grecian urns on the corner posts of the marital bed appeared a year later in the tips of the "spears" on the sheet metal canopy of the Jyväskylä Workers' Club building. The bed itself is basically a Renaissance four-poster, although the actual idea has come in all probability from a certain American low-post bedstead type; this is at least indicated by a cone or pineapple finial erased to give way to the urn in the detail drawing.[57] Even though this version by Aino and Alvar is not exactly perfect in shape — the separate cross-board at the foot of the bed does not quite fit the overall composition — with its aristocratic air it is, when seen in the original, absolutely astounding in appearance, especially when one remembers that originally it was intended to stand on a separate dais (!) The small tables belonging to the bed are, by comparison, considerably more conventional, the model being a tripod table of English type that has been almost semi-industrially manufactured in Scandinavia as early as the 18th century.[58]

The piece of furniture whose final form ultimately caused the greatest headache was the dressing table; at its most elegant it was like an altar with a row of shallow drawers parallelling the table top and a curtain concealing the lower part and the legs. As the designing progressed drawers were added below the top, and, when finally even the curtain was left away, the result had turned into an ordinary writing desk with "Dachshund" legs and side cupboards. And, to cap it, a mistake in the dimensioning had crept in: the whole piece had become so low that no room for the knees was provided. The wall mirror to go above it remained, however, to the end in accordance with the original conception, though the glass was not fitted in two parts in the 18th century fashion as had been proposed.

In execution this bedroom suite was typical of its period being made entirely from birch, stained dark brown, and polished. But about the other works of Aino and Alvar in the twenties to be discussed further on, only scant information has been transmitted as to the material used, the finishings, or the colours as the drawings very seldom make mention of such matters. Thus, for example, we know nothing of how they felt about the return of painted furniture, a fashion long absent, or about the colours then in vogue, *"the greyish-pink of a well-whisked lingonberry parfait", "the light green of verdigris"*, etc.[59] This is a real pity because the "colour problem" was of especial interest to professional people at that time, so much so that Gustaf Strengell in his *Koti taideluomana* (The Home as a Work of Art) 1923 devoted almost half the book to its analysis.

•

The design of the café interior made at the same time as the furniture for the classmate, was linked to an alteration and extension project on a property in Jyväskylä owned by the district Civil Guard which also has been commissioned from Alvar.[60] Two small wooden buildings at the corner of Kauppakatu and the present Gummeruksenkatu were combined with an additional building; the resulting large business premises were rented by the proprietor of the Seurahuone Café, who asked Alvar to do the complete furnishings.[61] Different types of tables and chairs were designed for each of the three consecutive rooms and, in addition, a service counter and cupboard in the first or fireplace room, tall mirrors on either side of the arched entrance to the middle or ladies' parlour, and an orchestra platform for the music or dining room at the back. Judging by the newspaper reports all this was carried out in one form or another though, in the absence of photographic evidence, it has to be evaluated on the knowledge gathered from the drawings alone.

THE FURNISHINGS FOR THE SEURAHUONE CAFÉ
IN JYVÄSKYLÄ,   1924

The furnishing of a public place provided an opportunity for experimenting with furniture that differed in dimension and form from the everyday environment.   a and b. Interior design by Aino and Alvar; cross-sectional sketch and reconstructed plan 1:50.   (A. fireplace room B. ladies' parlour C. dining room D. kitchen E. cabinet).   21

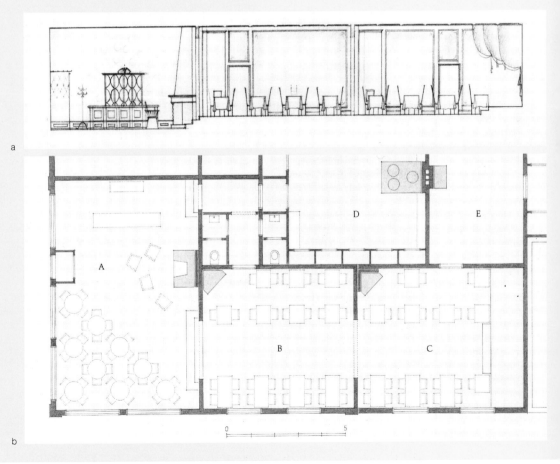

a

b

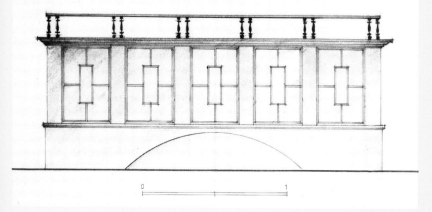

a

b

c

d

e

22 The service counter was composed like a building with favourite themes from different periods.   a and b. Design by Aino and Alvar; sketches 1:25 and 1:75.   c. Miniature balustrade used in 19th century Neo-Renaissance furniture.   d. The door panelling in a 16th century Renaissance sideboard.   e. Shallow segmental arch so beloved by the "Light Classicism" of the 1920's.

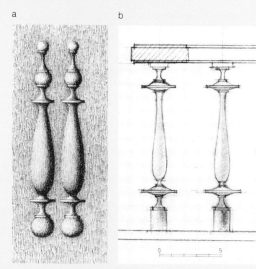

a

b

23

The pairing of the counter balusters and their shape are perhaps derived from the turned decoration on American furniture. a. "Split spindle" motif. b. Detail from working drawing, 1:3.

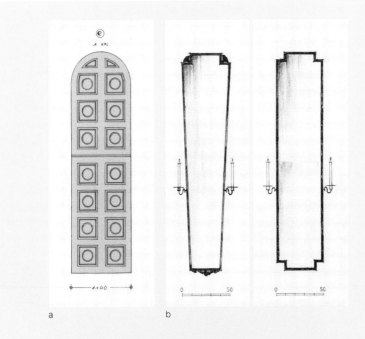

a

b

Characteristic of "Light Classicism" was the exaggerated vertical elongation of objects and shapes.   a. Seinäjoki Civil Guards' House main door from 1926, 1:66.6.   b. Designs for café mirrors by Aino and Alvar; sketches 1:40.   Cf plate 20.

24

25

The cupboard rising up behind the counter like a glass tower had borrowed its appearance from England.   a. A late 18th century Chippendale-style bookcase and one of the countless variations of glazing bar patterns, approx. 1:60.   b. Design by Aino and Alvar, sketch 1:30.

a

b

RITTER LIBRARY
BALDWIN-WALLACE COLLEGE

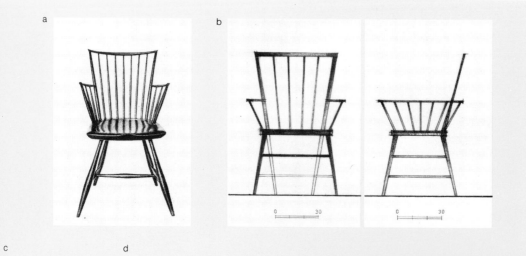

a

b

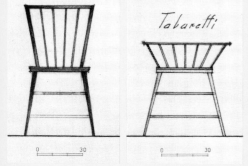

c

d

Tabaretti

26   A similarity to some earlier type of furniture can also be pure co-incidence.   a. American 19th century Windsor chair variant. b. Design for the host's chair by Aino and Alvar, sketches 1:25. c and d. Small chair and tabouret designed for the fireplace room, sketches 1:25.

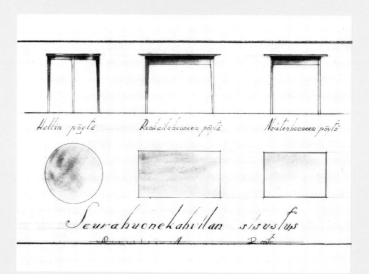

Hallin pöytä   Ruokailuhuoneen pöytä   Naistenhuoneen pöytä

Seurahuonekahvilan sisustus

The café tables designed by Aino and Alvar were practical but ordinary and similar to those already being manufactured. Sketches 1:50.

27

a

b

Classicism was in the 1920's a selfevident point of departure even in those furniture models that appeared abstracted or apparently freed from all stylistic dependence. a. American Chippendale-style sofa from the 1760's.   b and c. Chair designed by Aino and Alvar for the ladies' parlour; sketch 1:20 and illustration based on the working drawing.

28

c

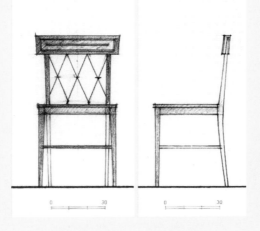

29

Even though the dining room chairs were the most classicistic in shape of all the furniture in the café, they do not appear to follow any definite model. Design by Aino and Alvar, sketches 1:20.

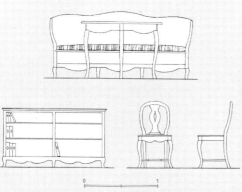

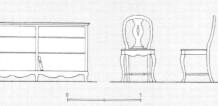

"Normal Classicism" favoured stylistic uniformity, but this usually meant buying all the furniture at the same time. Winning entry by W. West and E. Kyöstilä in the 1925 competition entitled, "The Living Room Furniture for a Small Home", 1:50.

30

31

One of the most cherished ideas of "Light Classicism" was the working in of a time effect in buildings and interiors in advance; the ideal was a home that had slowly taken shape over the years.   a. The sculptor C. Eldh's studio in Stockholm, designed by Ragnar Östberg in 1918, looked altered and enlarged already from the start; measurement drawing 1:400.   b. The Aaltos' own dining room in 1939 with furniture bought at different times.

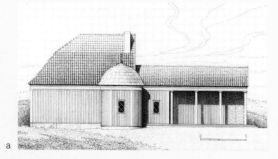

a

b

In their design for the interior of the Seurahuone Café, Aino and Alvar came, perhaps, closer to "Light Classicism" than in all of their other works; indeed the task did not even require any special dignity of expression, on the contrary it particularly suggested experiments in a lighter vein — even in the small-town somnolence of Jyväskylä something out of the ordinary was needed to arouse the interest of the customers.

The service counter and the crockery cupboard behind it were good examples of the intentional relationship between architecture and furniture design, for the counter, particularly, was composed and detailed like a building. The smooth lower part bordered by a horizontal batten was decorated by a flat segmental arch that was one of the most beloved plinth themes of the 1920's; because of the insufficiency of the drawing it is not known whether the arch was only a shallow recess or an opening through the counter (in the former version in architecture there was usually a small cellar window within the arch; the latter form was often used in supports for Dutch-tile stoves) [62]. The panels in the upper part of the counter framed by narrow bars bring to mind a row of windows, whereas the protruding moulding and the rail border with its double balusters resemble the eaves and roof balustrade. The same double baluster theme also appeared in full size, for instance, in the facades of the Jyväskylä Workers' Club (in the drawings sent for official inspection), and in a private villa in Kintaus. [63] The mischievousness characteristic of "Light Classicism" is seen in the irritatingly sparse positioning of these turned, miniature balusters, again, its unorthodox attitude to form in the fact that the whole idea of a table edge bordered with a balustrade was as such picked from the late 19th century "peg style" furniture which otherwise was despised above all. [64]

The crockery cupboard behind the counter which rose up like a glass tower was a variation of an English 18th century bookcase, with an enclosed lower part and the top as light as possible and vitrine-like in appearance. This elegance was achieved by using an intricately meandering pattern of filament-thin glazing bars on the doors giving the illusion of an airy "cobweb castle". This pattern, the same as on the front of the counter, originated as such from the realm of Renaissance forms, but here a new application had been found for it. [65]

Although "Light Classicism" in reality was more an attitude of mind than an actual uniform style, it also strove for a number of concrete objectives with regard to form. The more than two metre high yet only half a metre wide mirrors reflected one of these, perhaps the most typical one: the

fascination for exaggerated verticalism. This phenomenon naturally appeared in its most dramatic form in the macaroni-thin columns of the period, but it manifested itself generally in the favouring of all tall and thin shapes, be it letters, candlesticks, house gables, or room forms. In respect to mirrors one can, if one likes, add the association to the contemporary feminine ideal — the slender tomboy.

Each one of the rooms had a different set of chairs and tables, a fact which even aroused comment among contemporaries. [66] Yet in overall effect they were very similar to each other, all were characterized by an over-emphasized, almost under-dimensioned grace and fragility, a feature further accentuated by the wide meshed (cane?) backs of the chairs in the ladies' parlour and the music room. Still, when looking at the contemporary catalogues of the Muuramen Tuolitehtaan Oy and Wilh. Schaumanin Vaneritehdas Oy one notices that Aino and Alvar were, in fact, only following local tradition in their aim at lightness, especially as the chairs for the café were actually made in these same factories. [67] Even though the chairs in the music room are recognizable as distant relatives of the ancient Greek "klismos", the chairs in the ladies' parlour as influenced by the Chippendale-style, and those in the front room as a development from the Anglo-Saxon Windsor-chair, the Seurahuone Café models cannot be considered representative of any actual historical styles. Rather they already were abstracted "basic chairs" that in their clean-cut design and their firm proportions probably as such would have been suitable for mass production; in the circumstances only 20—30 pieces of each were made. [68]

•

In the summer of the same year Alvar received his third big interior design commission and this time Aino was also mentioned as an independent designer. [69] The Helsinki New Students' House had had two extra floors added to it; part of the new space was rented to the Häme Students' Society which turned to the Aaltos for the furnishings — probably because Alvar had been member of the Society. [70] As was his habit, he proposed a grandiose scheme far in excess of the client's resources with the result that the students moved their old furniture into the new premises and only had a part of the designs made. Although some newspaper pictures of the executed furnishings exist and, miraculously, a couple of the objects, it is again, for the analysis, best to turn to the drawings for a reliable image of the designers' ideas. [71]

The avoidance of a stylistic unity, seen in embryo in the Seurahuone Café, became almost programmatic in the Häme Students' Society. Aino and Alvar were no longer content that each room be furnished in a different spirit; now even the furniture within the same room could be of different pedigrees. In this case, at least, it worked beautifully as a disguising technique whereby a harmony was achieved between the new rooms and the old ones with their collection of rather undistinguished and mixed furniture. In "Normal Classicistic" interior design this was considered daring and as a method unsuitable at least to the layman as *"the best interior design is perhaps still achieved by using with sufficient vivacity the same style in the same room, in the same home, even in the same building".* [72] The endeavour towards a stylistic heterogeneity is, in fact, a reflection of a design principle most characteristic to "Light Classicism": the expressing of the strata of the past and the "projecting of history" into the work in advance. In other words, the architects wanted even a completely new building or room to look from the very beginning as if it had a long and varied life behind it. The master of this somewhat irrational game was Ragnar Östberg in his Stockholm Town Hall; his most charming creation in this field is, however, Carl Eldh's studio, made up of quite unmatched parts that lead the passer-by to think *"that this house once looked different and has now been added to".* [73]

The premises of the Häme Students' Society spread over two floors but the services of the interior designer was used only for the upper one. The spacious lounge Aino and Alvar left almost empty, limiting the furniture to a fixed seat running around the walls and designed like an Ostrobothnian chest-bench which, despite its frail back, seemed solid enough to withstand the wear and tear of student life. The rest of the furnishings consisted of a trestle table in the vernacular functioning as a serving counter, a separate chest, and five iron smoking tables, all looking like they had been salvaged from different furnishing stages in accordance with the principle described above. The most interesting in appearance are the smoking tables, the design inspiration having come from the picture of a Pompeian bronze table seen in a book on the history of furniture. [74] The purpose of the X-structure joining the legs had not, however, been correctly understood as the angle from which the picture had been taken did not show it clearly — originally this structure was part of a mechanism which allowed the table to be folded after the loose top had been removed, and thus it was not necessary in a fixed-legged table. In the first sketch the original Pompeian example had been so exactly copied that even the marble stand provided by the museum had been inadvertently included (!)

Probably for reasons of cost the complicated organic forms of the legs were simplified, and in the final, executed version the legs were made from round bar-iron with only the bottom parts forged into humorous "webbed feet". The table tops are of sheet metal, and the edges are turned up as in trays *) — a highly practical solution, for the lounge functioned unofficially (during Prohibition) as a kind of "Restaurant Tavastia".

It was not so very surprising that reality later copied art: when the Häme Students' Society in 1931 moved into new premises these same smoking tables were taken along and, once again, they gave the lounge the sought-for — but this time genuine — time perspective. [75]

In the auditorium the task given to Aino and Alvar was limited to designing the furniture for the "podium", the actual seats for the rest of the room coming from elsewhere. In the first draft, the chairmen's desk had been visualized as a huge Renaissance chest but was ultimately realized as an almost three-metre long table of the sturdiest model possible, which certainly came up to the expectations of the client with regard to ceremoniousness. Still, when looking now at this table one cannot avoid the impression that there were concealed some mental reservations in its intentionally pompous forms and military hauteur, perhaps a slight pique pointing to the Civil Guard spirit then prevailing in the Society. Three Renaissance chairs upholstered in brown imitation leather stood behind the table equal to it in their straight-laced solemnity; although the type is originally South European, Aino and Alvar appear to have used an American 17th century version of it as their model. [76] The staggeringly high wrought iron candelabrum intended to complete the effect at first sight appears to have been the unmatched element, but on reflection it was quite in keeping with the suite as exactly this kind of slender candelabra were used to light the massive tables standing in the centre of Renaissance halls. [77] (Alvar's somewhat surprising enthusiasm for wrought iron objects would appear to derive from the fact that he was the Jyväskylä agent for a Helsinki decorative arts smithy). [78]

---

*) It has since been discovered that the tables were originally painted in many colours: the feet in black with leaf ornaments and rings in brick-red and the table tops in verdigris. The deliberate childishness of this colour display is, of course, in the spirit of "Light Classicism". At the same time we get at least a partial answer to the earlier mentioned problem of the relationship of Aino and Alvar to the colours in fashion at the time.

THE FURNISHINGS OF THE HÄME STUDENTS' SOCIETY ROOMS, 1924

In furnishing the new floor of the Students' Society apartments every effort was made to avoid stylistic unity : the new furniture was meant to have the same homelike jumble of pieces of varying age as the old. Reconstruction of Aino's and Alvar's original design based on sketches, photos, and measurements, 1:200. (A. lounge B. auditorium C. men's clubroom D. ladies' clubroom). 32

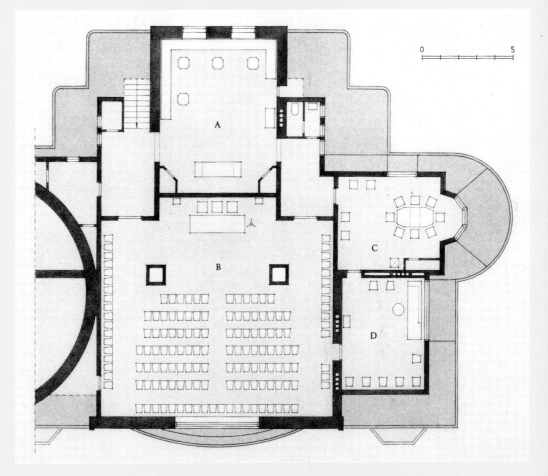

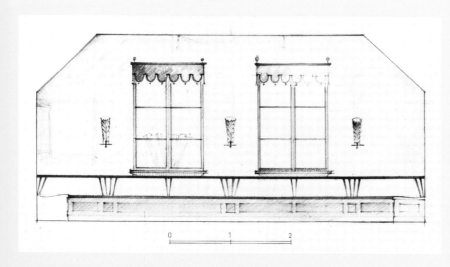

a

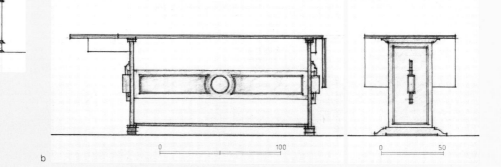

b

Although Aino and Alvar were not apparently very much interested in the "Folkloristic trend", the original idea for the chest bench around the walls of the lounge may well have come from a peasant house.   a. Cross-sectional sketch of the lounge, 1:60.
b. Ostrobothnian peasant interior, early 20th century.

33

a

b

34   The endeavour characteristic of Aino and Alvar to create "refined" interiors explains the Renaissance features and other stylistic additions to even rustic-type furniture.   a and b. Sketches of the lounge chest and trestle table, 1:30.

The excessive diagonal struts and "webbed feet" of the legs gave the iron smoking tables in the lounge the effect of "walking trays".

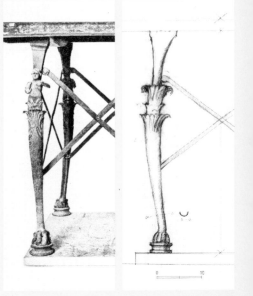

The smoking tables were deliberately designed to contrast the rusticity of the other furniture — the model being an ancient bronze table.   36
a. Pompeian table on its stand in the museum.   b. First sketch by Aino and Alvar, 1:8. c. Final sketches, 1:25. d. Measurement drawing of the executed table, 1:25.

a

b

c

d

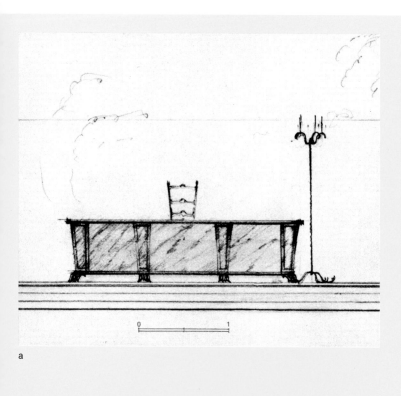

a

Alvar was the Jyväskylä agent for a Helsinki decorative arts smithy. a. Toivakka church candelabrum from 1923, measurement drawing 1:50. b. Candelabrum intended for the Jyväskylä Workers' Club from 1924. c. Candelabrum intended for the Students' Society auditorium, sketch 1:45.

a b c

The hierarchic importance of the table on the podium in the auditorium was conveyed by the style proposed for it. a. First design by Aino and Alvar, "gigantic Renaissance chest", sketch 1:40. b. Second, executed design, an almost three-metre long Renaissance table; sketches 1:33.3.

38

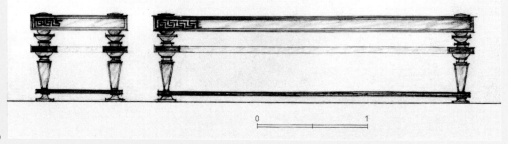

b

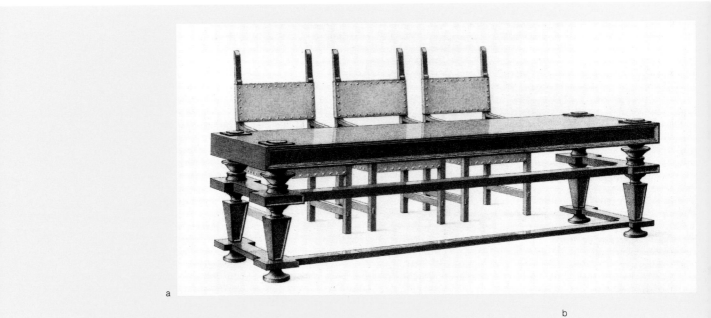

a

b

The pompous, military bearing of the table brings to mind the Civil Guard spirit prevailing also in student societies at that time — expressiveness based on a multiplicity of associations belongs naturally to Classicism.   a. Illustration based on photos of the executed table.
b. Example of a motif with clear militaristic associations: a Dioscures group intended for the Jyväskylä Civil Guards' House from 1927, 1:100.   39

a   b

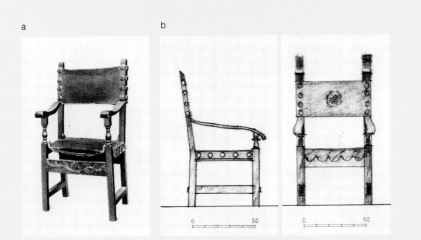

To ensure overall dignity even the chairs were of Renaissance type. a. American 17th century version. b. Chair design by Aino and Alvar, sketches 1:30.

40

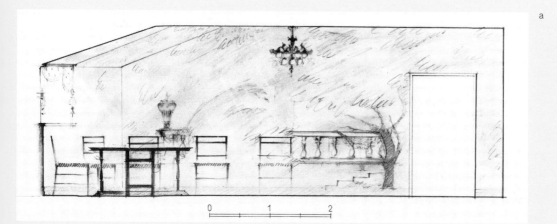

a

b

For the men's clubroom it was intended to revive one of the essential interior themes of Classicism : illusory painted scenic wallpaper.   a. Design by Aino and Alvar, cross-sectional sketch 1:60.   b. A room designed by David Gilly in 1798, Freienwald Castle.

41

a

42   The table standing in the middle of the "overgrown Italian garden" represented an Anglo-Saxon country atmosphere.   a. American late 17th century gate-leg table.   b. Design by Aino and Alvar, sketches 1:30.

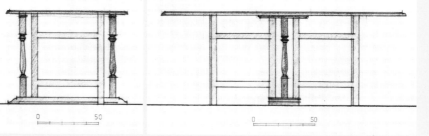

b

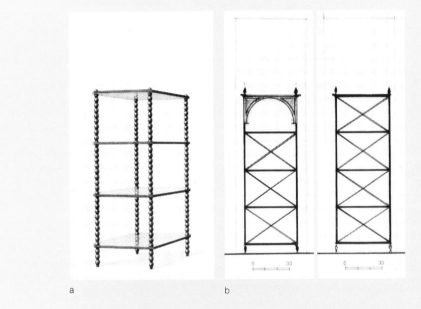

The basic form of the newspaper rack intended for the recess in the wall was one common in 19th century homes : the etagère.　　a. The whatnot from the home of the writer Z. Topelius.　　b. Design by Aino and Alvar, sketches 1:30.

43

The gnat-like, elegant chairs designed for the men's clubroom were also descendants of a long tradition.　　a. Early 20th century popular imported model, Latvian rustic chair. b and c. Design by Aino and Alvar; sketches 1:25 and illustration based on them.

44

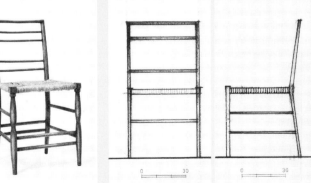

c

a

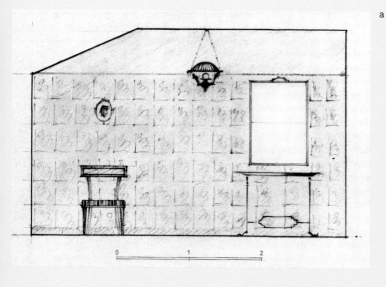

b

The austerity and ascetic impression often prevalent in "Light 45
Classicism" differed clearly from the ample forms and "bourgeois
snugness" of "Normal Classicism".   a. First sketch for the
ladies' clubroom by Aino and Alvar; cross-section 1:50.   b. Design for a lady's boudoir by J. S. Sirén from 1915.

46   The "roll-over arm" of the chaise longue was a stylistic feature of Anglo-Saxon
       18th century furniture design.   a. American Chippendale-style sofa,
       from the 1760's.   b. Design by Aino and Alvar, sketch 1:30.

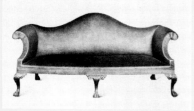

a

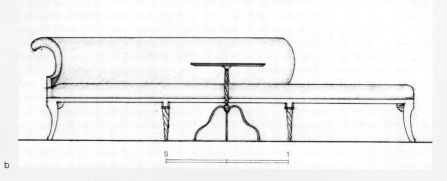

b

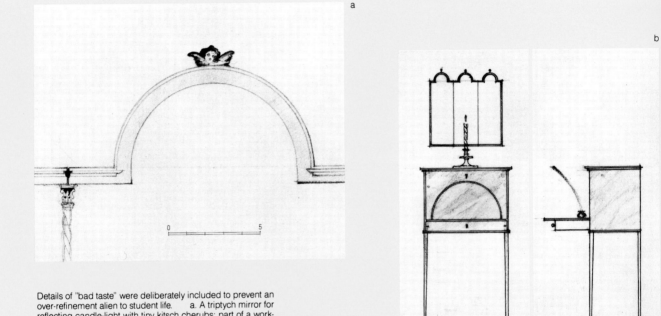

Details of "bad taste" were deliberately included to prevent an over-refinement alien to student life.   a. A triptych mirror for reflecting candle-light with tiny kitsch cherubs; part of a working drawing by Aino, 1:2.   b. The "precariously" harmonious and devout furniture group intended for the ladies' clubroom; sketches by Aino and Alvar, 1:25.   47

The cultural tradition of Ancient Greece adapted to Finnish university student surroundings.   a. Biedermeier version of the "klismos" chair, early 19th century.   b. Chair design by Aino and Alvar, sketches 1:25.

48

"AN ARTISTICALLY ARRANGED INTERIOR" II

a

b

As a classicistic building was basically always a kind of home for the gods, the ideal room interior was one without any furniture.   a and b. Competition entry by Aino and Alvar for the Jyväskylä rectory from 1926, perspective sketches of the hallway and chapel.

As everyday reality, however, demanded furniture, they were placed in tight groups along   50
the walls so as to preserve the impression of emptiness.   a. The Swede E. G. Asplund's sketch for a music room at an exhibition of interior design in 1920.   b. Furniture group in the home of the architect G. Strengell in the early 1920's, 1:50.

a

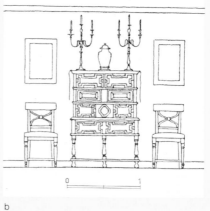

b

The men's clubroom had originally been conceived like a stage setting for some play: the walls had been painted to represent an overgrown garden complete with a balustrade-enclosed terrace, and out of this slightly melancholic lyricism there emerged, as from the morning mist, a gate-leg table and twelve chairs. The table was of an English 17th century type, though the actual example came from the American Colonial period (as before, this was due probably more to the meagre selection of books available to Aino and Alvar rather than any particular interest in America). [79] The chairs were extremely ascetic and almost gnat-like in dimensions; their inspiration had been a Latvian, rush-seated rustic model which at that time was a popular import into Finland. [80] Eliel Saarinen had dozens of them in his home in Hvitträsk and Alvar also owned a few, at least in the 1930's. [81] In addition the furnishings included a metal(?) newspaper rack or whatnot intended for a wall recess; its minimal amount of material is also a distinctive feature. The rational form of the rack was in itself nothing new, deriving as it did from the familiar 19th century étagère; only it was given a slightly more up-to-date air. The use of this type again indicates how wide and unbiased a repertoire of ideas Aino and Alvar possessed. All this elegance, regrettably, remained only on paper, for in actual fact a set of old deep, leather easy chairs and a rug-covered panel sofa were brought into the room, thus changing the atmosphere into one most snug and mundane.

If the cultivated effect envisaged for the men's clubroom remained but wishful thinking — the period of the deepest Prohibition was on — the restrained gentility planned by Aino for the interior of the ladies' clubroom was more founded on reality as female students at that time really were well-bred young ladies from respectable homes. The eight Biedermeier Style "klismos" chairs, now far closer to the originals than those in the Seurahuone Café, the long asymmetric chaise longue, and the round iron(?) table situated in front of the window formed the basic items of the furnishings. The evident frivolity of the chaise longue was balanced by the pious spirit of the group on the other side of the room: a slender-legged bureau with a three-part mirror above it. In its sure proportions and lightness, this writing desk was representative of "Light Classicism" based on late Gustavian form at its best; nothing could have been added or taken away. The already sacral spirit of the design was further enhanced by the dimly glowing pewter-framed mirror which opened like an altar triptych; the overall effect would have been refined and gracile almost to the point of irritation if the impression had not been let down by a deliberate manifestation of "bad taste": three tiny Ra-

phaelesque kitsch cherubs were peering down from the upper edge of the frame!

•

Aino and Alvar had hardly managed to bring the furnishing of the Häme Students' Society rooms more or less creditably to conclusion — Aino was still busy on the final working drawings as the students were moving in [82] — when already at the end of the year they entered a furniture design competition arranged by the Finnish Society of Crafts and Design. The object of the competition was to design the living room furniture for a family of small means, the bedroom interior was not included in the programme. [83] The organizers had, in all probability, expected entries in the "vackrare vardagsvara" spirit, unpretentious yet beautiful in form, possibly also based on the Finnish tradition. The joint entries of Aino and Alvar entitled "Trianon Americain" and "Monte Pie" were, however, from their very titles strangers to this objective and failed, in fact, to earn an award. [84] In the style of the Häme Students' Society rooms, the most eye-catching feature is again the stylistic heterogeneity of the various pieces; by this simple "trick" the impression was given of a highly individual and naturally evolving home in which the items have been purchased at different times and from different places. Conversely, the aim of those who won prizes had been a stylistically uniform set of furniture that at its worst created the furniture-store feeling of the "ideal home".

The models suggested by Aino and Alvar were all of them international borrowings: the original ideas for the cupboard, the chests of drawers, and the dining table are to be found in the book on American Colonial furniture already frequently mentioned; the chair was again a new variant of the Windsor type. The bookcase specified in the competition programme was conceived as an English office model which revolved round a central axle, a piece of furniture owned by, among others, Sigurd Frosterus, August Strindberg, and V. I. Lenin. [85] The mirror mounted within a border of engraved glass in a metal framework alluded to 18th century Venice; the finest example of this type of 1920's mirror is the one in the Royal foyer of the Stockholm Concert Hall. [86] The general tone of the Aalto entries showed thus high cultural consciousness and perhaps even some snobbishness, indicating that in the designers' mind the family of small means of the competition was rather nearer to the educated class than the workers, in other words, a family which suspiciously closely resembled the young Aaltos who had just returned penniless from their honeymoon in North Italy.[87] (The pseudonym *"Monte Pie"* is, of course, derived from Piemonte).

•

In the spring and summer of 1925 the furnishing of the Jyväskylä Workers' Club came up, but, probably due to the financial straits of those commissioning the building, there was no intention of having new furniture models designed. Only in respect to the lights did Alvar manage to talk the building committee round, and so most of these were his own designs and made in the Helsinki smithy mentioned before.[88] One of the standard chairs produced by the Muuramen Tuolitehtaan Oy, the Viennese-influenced No. 1, was chosen for the café and chairs of a linkable type intended for *"Moving Picture Theatres"* for the auditorium; for the rest they relied on existing pieces of furniture.[89]

After this there followed a long, quieter period in the furniture designing of Aino and Alvar, at least so it would appear from the evidence of their drawing archive. In reality they were most certainly still drawing some pieces of furniture every so often in addition to their other work, but the next time we meet them fully engrossed in the task of designing interiors is not until 1928 when they were creating the various furnishings for the Muurame church and the Lounais-Suomen Maalaistentalo Oy building. By this time they had, however, been converted to a new belief and no longer had any use for the vocabulary of Classicism; the new slogan was: *"Beauty is the harmony of purpose (function) and form."*[90]

•

After having followed the development of Aino and Alvar as furniture and interior designers in the spirit of Classicism, in parts even in great detail, we are still confronted with certain questions which, however essential they may be, are by no means easy to answer.

Although the Classicism of the 1920's was no longer strictly faithful in its commitment to its two and a half thousand year tradition, often merely indicating its forms, it was despite all still a style which to a very large extent was based on a familiarity with original examples. In architecture the re-

quired knowledge of historical styles came, of course, as a part of the curriculum; the history of architecture at the University of Technology was considered of professional importance as late as the end of the 1910's, though with the passing of the great Classicist, Professor Gustaf Nyström, the subject was already somewhat worn down and faded.[91] Furniture designing was, however, touched upon in the teaching only marginally even though it was considered to be within the realm of the architect's profession.[92] Where then did Aino and Alvar obtain the required special knowledge of styles?

Their possible literary sources can be discovered even now, afterwards, because it is fortunately relatively easy to reconstruct the range of relevant journals and books then generally available. On the other hand, it is considerably more difficult to bring forth, for instance, the everyday visual reality that surrounded them, in other words, the furniture on sale, the furnishings of homes and public buildings, the entire world of forms that inevitably also served as an inspiration.

The best source for information on current trends in furniture and interior designing were the professional journals — books on the other hand, were best for historical styles. At that time the library of the University of Technology subscribed, in addition to our own architectural journals, *Arkitekten* and *Arkkitehti*, naturally to the Scandinavian journals, the Swedish *Arkitektur* and *Byggmästaren*, the Danish *Architekten*, and the Norwegian *Byggekunst*, the latter, however, not until 1925[93], but these did not very often contain articles or illustrations on furniture design. Slightly more rewarding in this respect were the English *The Studio*, especially its yearbooks, the Austrian *Der Architekt* and *Kunst und Kunsthandwerk*, the German *Deutsche Kunst und Dekoration*, and the French *Art et Décoration* — the last we know Alvar to have at least flicked through[94]. Actual Scandinavian publications on the applied arts, such as the modest Finnish *Käsiteollisuus* or the Swedish *Konstslöjdföreningens tidskrift*, were not subscribed to by the University but they did go to the library of the Finnish Society of Crafts and Design which we can assume to have been known by an Ornamo member like Alvar; *Käsiteollisuus* was, in any case, familiar to Alvar because he occasionally contributed to it.[95]

One can also quickly list the books on the history of furniture in the University of Technology library, because at the time that Aino and Alvar were students there were in fact only three: A. Koeppen — C. Breuer: *Geschichte des Möbels* (1904), Fr. Lenygon: *Furniture in England from 1660 to 1760* (1914), and H. Havard: *Dictionnaire de l'ameublement*

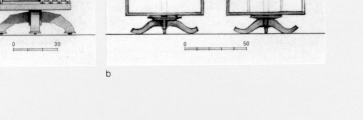

a   b

51

Space saving in a small home : an English revolving office bookcase which could contain up to a couple hundred volumes.   a. Imported model, early 20th century, 1:25.   b. Competition entry by Aino and Alvar (Trianon Americain), 1:30.

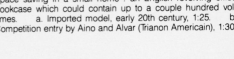

For the dining room suite the Anglo-Saxon vernacular served again as a model.   a. Swedish version of the Windsor chair from the 1920's.   b. Competition entry by Aino and Alvar (Tr.A.), chair 1:30.   c. American late 17th century gate-leg table.   d. Competition entry by Aino and Alvar (Tr.A.), dining table 1:30.

52

a b

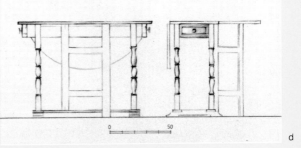

c   d

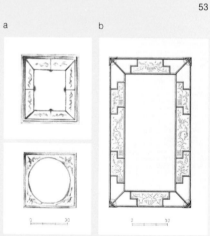

Even a small home needed some luxury.   a. Engraved mirrors of the competition entries by Aino and Alvar (Monte Pie and Tr.A.), 1:30.   b. The Swede Carl Malmsten's "Venetian mirror" from 1926, 1:30.

53

a   b

The "Queen Anne arches" of the cupboard and the "stonework" fronts of the chests of drawers indicated an origin in North America.   a. American late 18th century corner cupboard.   b. Competition entry by Aino and Alvar (Tr. A.), 1:30.   c. American late 17th century chest of drawers.   d. Competition entries by Aino and Alvar (Tr. A. and M. P.), 1:30.

54

a   b

c   d

et de la décoration, in four volumes; in addition to these there was P. A. Wells — J. Hooper: *Modern cabinet work furniture & fitments* (1909), which described methods of cabinet work. Prior to their departure for Jyväskylä the library had, moreover, acquired J. Lux: *Von der Empire- zur Biedermeierzeit* (1921) and the following volumes in the *Bauformen-Bibliothek* series: *Wohnungskultur und Möbel der italienischen Renaissance* (1921), *Möbel und Raumkunst in England 1680—1800* (1920), *Der Stil Louis XVI* (1913), and, the most important one of all, *Amerikanische Möbel der Kolonialzeit* (1917). [96]

Although at first glance this collection appears quite comprehensive, it includes no books, for instance, on the Gustavian Style, so vital from the point of view of "Light Classicism"; the explanation was simply that such books only appeared later on. [97] It is also worth noticing that certain works considered essential to the stylistic ideals of the 1920's — at least in retrospect — such as, Paul Mebes: *Um 1800* (1908, 2.ed. 1918), Heinrich Tessenow: *Hausbau und dergleichen* (1916), and Gregor Paulsson: *Vackrare vardagsvara* (1919) were not included in the new acquisitions made by the library of the University of Technology. [98] Conspicuously absent was also Alex. Koch's multi-volume series on new German interior art, *Handbuch neuzeitlicher Wohnungskultur*, a new edition of which had just been published at the end of the 1910's. [99] Thus developing a knowledge of the history of styles and catching the current flow of ideas depended greatly on one's own activeness. This the young Alvar did not lack, moreover, his alertness to perceive what was in the air was phenomenal; many of the surprising "hat tricks" performed in his works may be attributed precisely to this quick ability to look and adapt.

Were there any other ways in which Aino and Alvar could have acquired their knowledge? In respect to Alvar that which springs to mind is his foreign journeys. In 1920 he spent the whole summer in Sweden, mainly in Stockholm and Gothenburg, in 1921 on a stipend in the Baltic states, and in 1923 he was off again to Gothenburg, this time expressly for its Tri-Centennial Exhibition. [100] Unfortunately, we cannot know, except quite superficially, all that he saw on these visits or what in particular captured his attention. In any case, the Gothenburg Exhibition presented a broad view of contemporary Swedish applied arts and especially complete interiors; Alvar seems to have liked at least Carl Hörvik's high and bright hall, inasmuch as a picture of it appeared later on in one of his articles with the caption: *"An example of an elegant Swedish interior".* [101] During his period as an art critic Alvar was, on the other hand, re-

quired to cover the Finnish applied arts exhibitions, and some time later he even took part in them himself [102]; thus, it was not so very surprising that he was so thoroughly conversant with development at home and abroad.

Another important channel for non-literary influence was, of course, personal contacts. As to Aino we once again have little information, but judging from her design for the Finnish Society of Crafts and Design's lottery she must at least have had some contact with people in this field. Through his membership in Ornamo, Alvar, for his part, must certainly have known almost all of the contemporary "interior architects" from Arttu Brummer to Werner West, though in all probability his closest friend in these circles was, apart from Henry Ericsson, the director of the decorative arts smithy, Paavo Tynell. [103] In Sweden his most important contact at that time was the Gothenburg architect Sten Branzell, who, in addition to being a well-known glass designer, was also interested in furniture. [104]

"The results of all our works tell something of the maker, but the most uncorrupted truth is revealed by that which is closest to us, that which we do for ourselves, i.e. the home." [105] These words of Alvar suffice to form the basis for another question which inevitably arises, particularly in respect to architects. What expression did Aino and Alvar who, as professionals, designed furniture for their acquaintances and interiors for public buildings, give to their own home? Was it full of chairs and tables of their own creation, was it a test laboratory for prototypes, or was it, perhaps, just another typical Jyväskylä home furnished with Muuramen Tuolitehtaan Oy's dark-red, stained drawing room furniture complete with rocking chair? Of this, unfortunately, we know precious little, infuriating though it may be. One accidental glimpse is of Alvar's first bachelor rooms in Jyväskylä in 1923 — his combined bureau and home in the stone foundations of the wooden Town Hotel in Vapaudenkatu. [106] The next-door neighbour was the editorial office of *Sisä-Suomi*, the local organ of the Conservative Party, thus the following eloquent description has been preserved for succeeding generations in the paper's recollections of its first decade: *"We were truly modest lodgers. The press room at Sisä-Suomi contained a table, a chair, and a couple of wooden crates. The office was only slightly better equipped. The architect's bureau contained a couple of beds (as he had an assistent or so-called drudge), a table, and a couple of chairs as well as a few wooden crates."* [107] This sparseness of the furnishings need indicate, of course, no more than that Alvar's pecuniary situation, after his release from the army and the trip to Gothenburg, left something to be desired. It is unnecessary

to read into it portents of a Functionalist way of life or even seeing it as Tessenowian austerity.

•

We are now put to the task of presenting a cautious evaluation of the furniture and interior design work of Aino and Alvar against its contemporary Finnish background; cautious because our own overall picture of the period is still very unclear and limited. Neither is it worth while to compare their interior art to international standards, the Scandinavian countries apart, because it was still to a great extent sporadic and incidental to their main work.

By and large their work followed the general line then prevailing in Finland, which, in honour of the newly acquired independence, strove to create a Finnish identity in the applied arts and at the same time, by joining the Scandinavian Classicistic frontline, to dismantle the spiritual isolation caused by the wars. [108] As we have seen before, the question of national content did interest Alvar but more as a theoretical phenomenon; in his articles he could mention as a favourable development the trend which aimed at *"something homemade, more in the vein of our folkloristic past"* and gave as a good example the *Hihhulit* (Ecstatic religious meeting) painted by the artist Tyko Sallinen, a picture *"wholly built on the basis of old church paintings"*. Yet in the same breath he already warned against objects *"which have a feeling so steeped in Finnish antiquity that it is to be feared they are not suitable as furniture for our homes today"* [109], and in practice he and Aino very rarely adapted folk art to their works and even kept aloof from all kinds of *"cosy rag-rug styles"* then so much in demand among the experts. [110]

On the contrary, there is a clear striving in the interior art of Aino and Alvar towards an upper-class, cultivated expression, almost a pathetic desire to prove that Finland, too, was one of the heirs of European humanist culture. The truth is, of course, that the veneer of civilization in Finland was and still is very thin, far thinner than in either Sweden or Denmark. This perhaps is enough to explain why the handling of themes of Classicistic origin by Aino and Alvar did not achieve the same degree of refinement and ease as, for example, that of their contemporaries Kaare Klint, Uno Åhrén, and E. G. Asplund. The creation of art in the Classicistic spirit without binding oneself too much to its past forms can really succeed only on the basis of a long cultural tradition.

Also of significance is the fact that Aino and Alvar did not try to prove that Finland was linked to Europe by making use of contemporary furniture designs but rather turned directly to the older traditions. So one very seldom finds in their works reference to, for instance, German or French styles of the 1920's, [111] but instead direct borrowings from the form supplies of Ancient Rome, Renaissance Italy, or 18th century England. This tendency appeared to be common among architects in general and was undoubtedly due to their training; interior designers educated at the Central School of Applied Arts, on the other hand, could sometimes also follow Continental trends. To talented people like Aino and Alvar this partial detachment from "keeping up with the times" presented only advantages; their work preserved a fresh and unconventional touch as they did not have to worry, as anxiously as did the professional furniture designers, about what in each case was appropriate, popular, or a hit with the general public.

Unprejudiced and creative as they where, Aino and Alvar differed to their advantage from other interior designers, more productive but also more tethered by conventions; still they were not quite alone among their contemporaries in this respect as, for example, both Erik Bryggman and Yrjö Lindegren among the architects seem to have been able, when necessary, to achieve a comparable detachment — we only know too little of their furniture designs. [112] The standard of Aino's and Alvar's output in this period did not, thus, surpass that of the others, as it was to do a few years later, although there were sporadic indications of just those characteristics upon which their future successes would be based: an ability to see things from new and unexpected angles and the skill to daringly unite ideas derived from different sources.

What position then did the period of the twenties occupy in the production of Aino and Alvar Aalto? In accordance with the outdated Giedionist historical view, which regards Functionalism as the highest stage of development, the only possible value this period could have had was as a warming-up phase prior to the onset of the golden age. In the eyes of the supporters of this view Classicism has been condoned only because its occasional bursts of ascetism could be accepted as evidence that it was on the right road towards that prime display of maturity: the standard form. In reality, each style period has, naturally, its own absolute value which is independent of preceding or succeeding trends in development and their changing value systems. Thus the meaning of the early works of Aino and Alvar lies somewhere else than in serving as a "jumping-off board".

Alongside the triumphant march of Functionalism, methods of design practice were destroyed at the same rate as new ones were created. The most significant losses were suffered in expressiveness. Where formerly designers had been able and also willing to give, for example, to each room its own individual character and atmosphere: romantic or festive, lyrical or stylish, and where even a touch of humour or irony had been added when required, within the new vocabulary of form and way of thinking such possibilities were severely restricted; what mainly remained was a democratic and uniform dullness. Against this background the interior design of Aino and Alvar in the 1920's should be rated even higher than at first perhaps appears necessary. Although this work had by no means as great an impact as that of the following decade, it still showed up a considerable number of professional methods and important human dimensions which could not be found later, either in the art of the Aaltos or in that of others. A feature which one misses most from their later, undeniably more balanced and finished works, is that daring versatility and stylistic colourfulness which threatened the limits of "good taste". Even though it was to a large degree the result of youth itself, we can still congratulate succeeding generations on the fact that their most sensitive developmental stage coincided with such a style period which still was deliberately based on the richness of expression.

•

The Classicistic interlude in the applied arts in Scandinavia only lasted some twenty years. [113] Although the older generation, whose youth and maturity had been spent under the reign of Jugend, had quietly come over to the side of Classicism, it could not, however, wholeheartedly believe in this new spring. In introducing in 1920 one of the most important Swedish furniture exhibitions of the time — it included works by, among others, E. G. Asplund and S. Lewerentz — the middle-aged Lars Israel Wahlman crystallized in a few lyrical lines the innermost essence of the whole period, the lurking presence of death under the surface. *"A game, but why? In an age that is slowly setting one has the habit to play games. The gold glittering leaves of summer left behind dance on the path that leads to the future. Thus autumnal art plays with the leaves of days past, already shed by the trees."* [114] The younger generation, those whose professional careers were initially framed by Classicism, seemed to have regarded it with a healthy

heartlessness and directness. They did not appear to see the tragedy concealed in their works, as did the outsider Wahlman, for what was to them more or less commonplace was in reality the final consummation of a long tradition. As long as Classicism was the dominant trend, the young scarcely stopped to question its right to existence, still less to ponder its loss when the new ideologies took power. Alvar at least took quite an indifferent stand to his own "yester-years" already by the autumn of 1928; with no pangs of conscience about his rejection of Classicism, he answered an interviewer enquiring about the new expression in domestic surroundings: *"We have passed that time when the furnishing of the home was considered a separate task based on sentimental concepts of form. The period through which we have gone was of particular significance in that it was said to have reawakened the desire for cosiness and the artistically balanced aesthetic concepts of taste in the old style periods. It is quite clear that this era that has just passed has been, to a certain extent, beneficial, but its sum total has not been the further development of this sense of style but, on the opposite, the complete relinquishing of what in everyday language is meant by style, in other words: we have arrived at a healthy goal, relinquished decorative form thinking in home interiors."* [115]

Although this statement by Alvar Aalto strictly speaking only refers to the furnishing of the home, it could be generalized to cover his view of all interior art. It contains no apparent condemnation of the Classicistic period which was, in his mind, a thing of the past (in reality Classicism continued to flourish in Finland well into the 1930's), but neither does it suggest that it had given him, or others, any useful skill or knowledge. There comes to mind the similar fate of film art in the same years: with the coming of the new means of expression, sound, it seemed that all the knowledge gained by toil and agony was forgotten in a flash, and it took a long time before an artistic equilibrium was again achieved. The same thing seems to have happened to architecture as well as to furniture and interior design; when designers were caught in the ecstasy of the new truths of Functionalism, much irreplaceable experience was thrown overboard: so-called timeless ideas, sense for nuances, and possibilities for variation, in other words, all that which is valid forever and everywhere. Now, after 50 years, it is actually all too easy to see that the wheel had turned full circle, that designers were, in fact, back in the same position whence they had begun when young; behind them a stylistic ideal now exhausted, before them a new one waiting to be exploited, yet containing all the possibilities of new and unforeseen mistakes.

8. A talk, illustrated with "magic lantern" slides, was held at the Jyväskylä University Association on 6.3.1925 and it was also heard over the newly begun local radio service.

    Sisä-Suomi 7.3.1925, p.1, "Jyväskylän Yliopistoyhdistyksen juhlailtama" and p.3, "Jyväsk. Yliop.yhdistyksen eilisen juhlan ohjelma". *Sisä-Suomi* 8.3.1925, p.3, "Akateemisessa hengessä".

9. Alvar's desire for publicity was ridiculed by Gustaf Strengell in a light parody in which he "quoted" an article praising Alvar in an imaginary American architectural journal called *The Architectural Tomfoolery* and gave to understand that this article had been *"if not actually supplied by Mr Aalto himself then at least inspired by him".*

    Hufvudstadsbladet 10.7.1932, p.9. Gustaf Strengell: "Alvar Aalto, Finlands första funktionalist".

10. STKK (The Finnish University of Technology), minutes of the "Opettajakollegi" for 1931, meeting of 10.3.1931, § 7; HTKK (The Helsinki University of Technology) Archives.

11. Professor Onni Tarjanne's expert opinion given on 22.1.1931.

    STKK, minutes of the "Opettajakollegi" for 1931, meeting of 10.3.1931, § 7, enclosure; HTKK Archives.

12. *Keskisuomalainen* 22.1.1925, p.3, Alvar Aalto: "Eräs kaupunkimme kaunistustoimenpide ja sen mahdollisuudet".

13. Interview with the architect Kerttu Tamminen, 11.6.1977.

14. *Arkkitehti* 1922/2, p.25, Alvar Aalto: "Menneitten aikojen motivit".

15. *Iltalehti* 12.12.1921, p.7, A.A.-o: "Greta-Lisa Jäderholm".

16. *Aamulehti* 26.6.1922, p.4, Alvar Aalto: "Teollisuusnäyttelyn rakennustaiteellinen puoli".

17. *Helsingin Sanomat* 25.4.1921, p.3, Alvar A.: "Ornamon näyttely".

18. *Jyväskylän työväentalo, tupaantuliaisiin 12. —13.9.1925*, Jyväskylä 1925, p.38, Alvar Aalto: "Muutamia rakennustaiteellisia suuntaviivoja".

19. See Note 15.

20. See Note 18.

21. Björn Linn: *Osvald Almqvist, en arkitekt och hans arbete*, Stockholm 1967, p.41.

22. *Wilh. Andstens fabriks-aktiebolag — Wilh. Andstenin tehdas-osakeyhtiö* [illustrated catalogue of Dutch-tile stoves], Helsinki 1912.

23. For example, *Suomen koristetaiteilijain liitto Ornamo, vuosikirja II*, Porvoo 1927, p.18, Arttu Brummer: "Kodin taiteellisesta huolittelusta".

24. The set of bedroom furniture designed by the architect Werner von Essen.

    Huonekaluja — Möbel (Kansanvalistusseuran käsiteollisuuspiirustuksia n:o 2), [1911], p.9. *Huonekaluja, neljäs sarja* (Tietosanakirjaosakeyhtiön käsiteollisuuspiirustuksia n:o 13), Helsinki 1924, p.5.

25. The then model No. 50 made by the Lahden Puusepätehdas Oy company. Exactly the same set was also manufactured by the Juho Konttinen Oy company.

    Riitta Miestamo: *Asko Osakeyhtiön huonekalumallistoa vuosilta 1918—1973* (MA thesis in 1973 at the Faculty of Art History, University of Helsinki), p. 11. *Juho Konttinen Osakeyhtiö, Kuopio* [furniture catalogue, s.a.], No. 60.

26. *Muuramen Tuolitehtaan Osakeyhtiö, kuvasto n:o 6*, Jyväskylä 1919. *Wilh. Schaumanin Faneeritehdas Oy, huonekaluja*, [c. 1925].

27. In Sweden at least David Blomberg Ab produced copies of furniture in the Nordiska Museet's collection; no precise information is available on similar cases in Finland though in all probability they existed.

    David Blomberg, Stockholm [furniture catalogue], Malmö 1927, p.42.

28. *Käsiteollisuus* 1927/1—2, p.23, Arttu Brummer: "Taideteollisuus 'Käsiteollisuuden' palstoilla".

29. *Koristetaiteilijain liitto Ornamo, vuosikirja 1927*, Porvoo 1927, p.11, Rafael Blomstedt: "Suomen taideteollisuus ja Koristetaiteilijain liitto Ornamo".

30. *Suomen Kuvalehti* 1929/1, p.22, Gustaf Strengell: "Kerettiläisiä mielipiteitä huonekaluista".

56

1. As far as is known at present, the three-legged stool was exhibited for the first time in November 1933 in London. Apparently it had not as yet been displayed at the Triennale in Milan in the summer of that same year nor at the Building Congress for the Nordic Countries at Helsinki in 1932; so called Paimio chairs of plywood, on the other hand, had been already seen both in Milan and at Helsinki.

    The Architects' Journal 9.11.1933, pp. 587—588, "Finland and England", and 16.11.1933, pp. 627—630, "Exhibition of Finnish Furniture". Harry Röneholm: *Markkinat, messut ja näyttelyt I*, Helsinki 1945, p.305. *Arkkitehti* 1932/7, p.106—107, Yrjö Laine: "Tyyppivalmistenäyttely".

2. "Keski-Suomen rykmentin sotilaskantakirja n:o 1, 1919—1925"; War Archives.

3. In 1920 Alvar drew some captioned cartoons for the Helsinki comic paper *Kerberos* and in the following year wrote seven causeries under the pseudonym *"Ping"*; they were illustrated by himself and the drawings were signed *"Alvar 20"* or *"Alvar 21"*. In the 1922/13 issue of *Ylioppilaslehti* there were a few of his caricatures of well-known students of technology.

    Alvar was the permanent visual and applied arts critic for the Helsinki paper *Iltalehti* as well as a commentator on architectural matters from November 1921 to April 1922. He wrote 31 articles during this period, usually signing them *"A.A-o"*.

4. On 11.10.1923 the Hanko company Oy Granit Ab entered into an agreement with Alvar whereby he would be their agent in Jyväskylä. Alvar inserted an appropriate advertisement in *Sisä-Suomi* on 21.12.1923 promising *"Artistic gravestones (...) in special cases designed by the architect Aalto".* His relationship with the company had begun in the winter of 1920 when the Alajärvi War memorial designed by Alvar was ordered from Hanko.   See also Note 42.

    The agreement of representation, cover No. 36 "Brev 1923 II"; the order for the War memorial, "Beställningsbok 1916—1921", p. 97; Oy Granit Ab's archives in the Åbo Akademi Library.

5. In the spring of 1922 Alvar was not only secretary to the board of SAFA (Association of Finnish Architects) but also secretary of its Helsinki branch; he had been accepted as a member of the Association on 25.11.1921.

    Minutes of meetings and annual report for 1922; SAFA archives. *Arkkitehti* 1921/6, p.16 and 1922/2, p.31.

6. Alvar was a member of the board of Ornamo in 1921 and an alternate member in 1922; he had been accepted as a member on 1.2.1920.

    "Konstindustriförbundet Ornamo, mötesprotokoll 1919—1925", meeting of 1.2.1920, § 8, meeting of 7.11.1920, § 9 and meeting of 6.11.1921, § 4; Ornamo archives.

7. Alvar was a supernumerary building surveyor appointed by the Jyväskylä Magistrates' Office, in actual fact its "architect member", from April 1926 to February 1927; the permanent members at that time being the editor-in-chief of *Keskisuomalainen*, the magistrate H. Hyppönen, and the town engineer E. J. Järvilehto. As an example of how Alvar took his job is a surveyors' certificate dated 25.10.1926 on which he has entered a diverging opinion: *"I consider myself (...) compelled to propose the rejection of these drawings above all because the location of the building on the most prominent side of this impressive square and the public character of the building would require a more developed facade design in better taste."*

    Jyväskylä Magistracy minutes for 1926 and 1927; Jyväskylä Provincial Archives.

31. *Arkkitehti* 1921/sample copy, pp.14—15, Gustaf Strengell: "Werner West".

32. The macabre keyhole is in the outer door to the funeral chapel in Stockholm's southern cemetery (Skogskyrkogården) drawn by E. G. Asplund in 1918—1920. The pillar and the baluster standing beside it appear in Alvar Aalto's sketch of J. F. Karpio's villa in Jyväskylä in 1923.

    Drawings; Aalto archives.

33. *Arkkitehti* 1924/5, p.67, Nils Wasastjerna: "Ruotsinmaalainen taide-teollisuusnäyttely".

34. *Arkkitehti* 1949/1—2, p.3, "Aino Aalto in memoriam".

35. Aino had commenced her studies in the autumn of 1913, three years before Alvar.

    Aino Marsio's diploma from the Architectural Department of STKK, dated 20.1.1920; HTKK Archives.

36. Interview with Hanna-Maija Alanen (née Aalto), 17.8.1982.

37. The drawings for the furniture had been commissioned from Aino in spring 1922, wood work was made at the Sörnäinen Penitentiary and the fabric for the upholstery woven at the Suomen Käsityön Ystävät Oy company. The whole set was displayed at the annual exhibition of the Finnish Society of Crafts and Design held at the Ateneum Gallery in late November and early December, lotted out and won by the Tampere businessman Anton Hahl and still remains in the possession of his family.

    "Konstflitföreningen i Finland, protokoll 1922", meeting of 26.5.1922, § 4 and meeting of 16.12.1922, § 1; The Finnish Society of Crafts and Design archives.   *Uusi Suomi* 29.10.1922, p.10, "Suomen taideteolli-suusyhdistyksen taideteollisuus- ja arpajaisvoittonäyttely".

38. Alvar *"entered military service"* officially on 1.6.1922 and was *"released from active service"* on 10.7.1923, but in actual fact spent almost half a year on leaves of different kinds, because his participation in the Civil War in 1918 counted in his favour. For example the Tampere Cottage and Small Industry Exhibition designed by Alvar was not opened until the end of June 1922, yet he was in charge of the building until it was ready.

    "Keski-Suomen rykmentin sotilaskantakirja n:o 1, 1919—1925"; War Archives.

39. The furniture was drawn for the elder brother of a classmate from the Jyväskylä Lyceum, the dentist Paavo Peräinen (1894—1968), but apparently never carried out.

    Jyväskylän Lyseo 1858—1933, Porvoo 1933, p.390.   Drawings; Aalto archives.

40. Drawings; Aalto archives.

41. Alvar designed the sections for at least following firms: Helsingfors Pip-och leksaksfabrik Ab, A. Fredrikson Oy (Jyväskylä) and Kotimaan lak-kitehdas Oy (Viipuri); he was awarded the Ornamo propaganda committee's diplomas for these.

    Helsingin Sanomat 7.7.1920, p.3, "Suomen messut, Diploomeja näytteillepanijoille".

42. Both Alvar Aalto and Henry Ericsson (1898—1933) were assistants to the architect Carolus Lindberg when he was planning the buildings for the Tivoli area of the Finnish Fair. Independently, the *"Taideteollisuus-toimisto Aalto & Ericsson"* designed at least the pavilion for the Hanko company Oy Granit Ab at the same Fair. Otherwise little is known of this Alvar's first bureau; later on it was mentioned only in the list of qualifications of one of his applications for a stipend.

    Ilkka 26.6.1920, p.7, "Suomen ensimmäiset kauppamessut".   The Ab Konstslöjd & Taidetyö Oy company's contract for building of the pavilion dated 27.5.1920, cover No. 31 "Brev 1920"; Oy Granit Ab's archives in the Åbo Akademi Library.   A. Aalto's application for a stipend, "Tekniska Högskolan i Finland inkomna expeditioner 1921", n:o 21/148 Sd 1921; HTKK Archives.

43. It would appear that Aino first came to work for Alvar in the winter of 1924; she had, however, lived in Jyväskylä throughout the preceding year and had been a draughtswoman in the private office of G.A. Wahlroos (1890—1943), the architect to the Wilh. Schaumanin Vaneritehdas Oy company. During this period Aino had, for example, done the final drawings and perspectives for the great steps on the Harju.

    Drawings; Jyväskylä Town Building Office archives.

44. Valter Wahlroos (1901—1968) was a decorative painter trained at the Central School of Applied Arts; he had helped out in the execution of the Tampere Cottage and Small Industry Exhibition in 1922 and made also the ceiling paintings from Alvar's sketches for the Toivakka church in the summer of 1923; he was apparently still an assistant in Alvar's first bureau in Jyväskylä in the autumn of the same year.

    Aamulehti 26.6.1922, p.4, Alvar Aalto: "Teollisuusnäyttelyn rakennustai-teellinen puoli".   *Keskisuomalainen* 16.10.1923, p.2, "Pikipäin Toiva-kan uusitussa kirkossa".   Interview with Mrs. Sedkil Wahlroos, June 1980.

45. Aino had worked during her student years in 1919 in the office of the landscape gardener Bengt M. Schalin (1889—) where she independently designed, for instance, the terraces and pavilion for the Villa Grankulla in Ytterö.

    Drawings; Museum of Finnish Architecture.

46. Immediately after he had graduated in spring 1921 Alvar acquired a drawing stamp with the legend ARKIT. ALVAR AALTO — this is what I have called the "small stamp". In December 1923 a new "large stamp" was taken into use which contained the same text in bigger letters, and a separate, rectangular "box-stamp" in which the particulars of the job and the initials of the draughtsman were filled in by hand.

47. The furniture had been ordered by a classmate of Alvar's from the Jyväskylä Lyceum, Erkki Peräinen, M.A., agronomist (1898—1930). In its executed form it consists of a double bed, two bedside tables, a wardrobe, a linen chest of drawers, a dressing table complete with mirror and two chairs, a tabouret, and a table; the last four items do not appear in the drawings made by Aino and Alvar and so could have been designed by the craftsman employed to make the furniture. The furniture remains in the possession of the family.

    Jyväskylän lyseo 1858—1933, Porvoo 1933, p.404.   Drawings; Aalto archives, Peräinen archives.

48. *David Blomberg, Stockholm* [furniture catalogue], 1922, p.22.   *Harald Westerberg, Linköping* [furniture catalogue], 1923, p.13.

49. Marshall Lagerquist: *Georg Haupt, ébéniste du Roi* (Nordiska Museets handlingar 92), Stockholm 1979, pp. 137—140, 156.

50. Gregor Paulsson: *Vackrare vardagsvara*, Stockholm 1919, p.9.

51. The sewing table designed by E. G. Asplund was displayed at the Verkstaden's Interior Exhibition in the Liljewalch's Art Gallery in Stockholm in the autumn of 1920; it was manufactured by David Blomberg Ab. Werner West's version was on display at the Koti-teollisuus Oy Pirtti company's Tenth Annual Exhibition in Helsinki in autumn 1921.

    Arkitektur 1920/12, p.163, L. I. Wahlman: "Rumskonsten på 'Verksta-dens' utställning".   *David Blomberg, Stockholm* [furniture catalogue], 1922, p.21.   *Suomen Kuvalehti* 1921/45, p.1107, "Päivän-kuvia".

52. The step-like structure of the American highboy was intended for the display of china; it did not have drawers as had the version designed by Aino and Alvar.

    L. V. Lockwood: *Colonial Furniture in America, Vol. I*, London — New York 1913, p.91. The same book in the STKK Library was the German edition *Amerikanische Möbel der Kolonialzeit*, Stuttgart 1917.   See also Note 93.

53. These Gustavian Style metal handles appearing in the drawings were not made; those in the realized piece of furniture are turned wooden knobs.

54. This leg shape belongs, of course, originally to the French Louis XVI, the model for the Swedish Gustavian Style.

55. Paul David Pearson: *Alvar Aalto and the International Style*, New York 1978, p.34.

56. *Arkkitehti* 1954/3—4, p.52, Alvar Aalto: "Näyttely NK:ssa Tukholmassa".

57. L. V. Lockwood: *Amerikanische Möbel der Kolonialzeit* (Bauformen-Bibliothek X), Stuttgart 1917, p.168.   Drawings; Peräinen archives.

58. *Form* 1933/6, pp.134—135, Gösta Selling: "Serie och standard på 1700-talet".

59. *Käsiteollisuus* 1923/5, p.63, Arttu Brummer-Korvenkontio: "Pyhiinvael-lusmatkalla Göteporiin II".

60. Kauppakatu 15 — Torikatu 11 (now Gummeruksenkatu), Jyväskylä I/14/2 (now I/14/10).

Drawings; Jyväskylä Town Archives.

61. The proprietor of the Seurahuone Café was the businessman Herman (Herkko) Wehmas (1865—1934). The café was opened on 19.10.1924, but rather surprisingly the newspapers made no mention at all of Alvar's share, yet, for instance, reported the window dressings by the sculptor O. Raja-Aho.

Keskisuomalainen 19.10.1924, p.3, "Seurahuone-kahvila". *Sisä-Suomi* 19.10.1924, p.2, "Seurahuone-kahvila avataan tänään". Drawings; Aalto archives.

62. This typical theme of the 1920's appeared for the first time in the plan for the Helsingborg Crematorium by S. Lewerentz and T. Stubelius in 1914 where it took the form of an opening going through the building. In this form it was also used in E. G. Asplund's Dutch-tile stoves and in the Dane Edward Thomsen's sofas. The best known example of the theme in its second version is the shallow recess in the foundations of the Villa Snellman designed by E. G. Asplund, but it is also present in the architecture of S. Lewerentz, H. Ekelund etc.

Arkitektur 1914/10, p.118. *Arkitektur* 1917/11, p.155. *Arkitektur* 1919/12, p.154. *Architekten* 1922, p.143. *Architekten* 1923/12, p.193. *Hufvudstadsbladet* 20.10.1927 p 3, etc.

63. This theme is no longer present in the executed version of the Jyväskylä Workers' Club, where the balusters are evenly spaced. The summer villa at Kintaus is that of the station master Oskari Tuurala (1871—1951), built around 1925.

Drawings; Alvar Aalto Museum, Jyväskylä and Aalto archives.

64. Miniature balustrades were already used in furniture in the 16th Century, but they only became typical in the Neo-Renaissance of the late 19th century, particularly in its Russian form. The most famous example of a table with a balustrade around the edge is Leo Tolstoy's writing desk in the Tolstoy Museum in Moscow.

65. English 18th century bookcases and china cabinets always had highly decorative and complex glazing bars on their glass doors, but the pattern used in the Seurahuone Café originates elsewhere; during the Renaissance it was used on coffered ceilings and the panelled doors of cupboards and wardrobes; the Neo-Renaissance wardrobes and desks in the House of Estates in Helsinki carry this form theme. The pattern became very popular in the 1920's and it could be used almost anywhere, from lift doors to market square cobbling.

Hermann Schmitz: *Das Möbelwerk*, Berlin [1926], p.91.

66. *Keskisuomalainen* 19.10.1924. p.3, "Seurahuone-kahvila".

67. Other companies employed in the interiors were Juho Konttinen Oy of Kuopio and Aug. Parkkosen puusepän ja verhoilijanliike of Jyväskylä. See Note 66.

68. Drawings; Aalto archives.

69. *Sisä-Suomi* 24.8.1924, p.1, "Hämäläis-Osakunta".

70. Although a student of technology, Alvar also belonged to the Häme Student's Society which he joined immediately upon matriculating in spring 1916. For some reason or other, he had to re-apply for membership in autumn 1918; he was then a keen participant in the Society's activities, giving a talk, among other things, on Eliel Saarinen's plan for "Suur-Helsinki".

"Hämäläis-Osakunnan pöytäkirjoja 15.2.1916—6.3.1917", meeting of 29.5.1916, § 1; "Hämäläis-Osakunnan pöytäkirjoja 6.3.1917—27.4.1919", meeting of 3.10.1918, § 1 and meeting of 12.11.1918, § 8; Helsinki University Library.

71. Aino and Alvar designed all the furniture for the Häme Students' Society's lounge, auditorium, men's clubroom and ladies' clubroom; only the first two were carried out with certainty; on the other hand, of the latter's men's clubroom, at least, remained just a plan. Today the Society only has the five smoking tables from the lounge and the three chairs from the auditorium in its possession.

Ylioppilaslehti 1925/16, pp.278—280, Huck Finn: "Hämäläis-Osakunnan uusi huoneusto". *Kaikuja Hämeestä IX*, Tampere 1929, illustrated supplement. Drawings: Aalto archives.

72. *Käsiteollisuus* 1925/1, p.6, Sisustusarkkitehti: "Kodinsisustus Englannissa".

73. *Arkitektur* 1919/12, p.144, Folke Bensow: "Carl Eldhs atelje".

74. Alfred Koeppen — Carl Breuer: *Geschichte des Möbels*, Berlin — New York 1904, p.207. See also Note 93.

75. The table and chairs from the auditorium were also removed to the new Häme Students' Society building designed by Elias Paalanen (now Urho Kekkosen katu 4—6).

Arkkitehti 1933/2, p.18, Elias Paalanen: "Hämäläisten talo". A. Pietinen's photograph No. 3191; National Board of Antiquities and Historical Monuments.

76. L. V. Lockwood: *Amerikanische Möbel der Kolonialzeit* (Bauformen-Bibliothek X), Stuttgart 1917, pp.117—118. See also Note 93.

77. Frida Schottmüller: *Wohnungskultur und Möbel der italienischen Renaissance* (Bauformen-Bibliothek XII), Stuttgart 1921, pp. 16, 18. See also Note 93.

78. Alvar was the Jyväskylä agent of the company Oy Taito which at that time had specialized in wrought iron objects and became later the leading manufacturer of functionalist lamps in Finland. In *Sisä-Suomi* on 16.12. and 21.12.1923 Alvar ran advertisements for the company; they offered "artistically and technically guaranteed industrial art, (...) works based on the smithy's own or Alvar Aalto's designs". See also Note 103.

79. L. V. Lockwood: *Amerikanische Möbel der Kolonialzeit* (Bauformen-Bibliothek X), Stuttgart 1917, p.84. See also Note 93.

80. *Eesti talupoja toolid*, Tartu 1969, p.6, photo 42.

81. *Arkitekten* 1909/6, pp.126—127 photos. *Arkkitehti* 1976/7—8, p.41 photo 1.

82. Aino's signature on the drawing of the mirror, for instance, is dated November 1924, but the students had already moved into their new premises by the end of October.

Drawings; Aalto archives. *Uusi Suomi* 23.10.1924, p.3, Kokouksia: "Hämäläis-Osakunta, muuttotalkoot".

83. The competition closed on 7.1.1925; the judges were Armas Lindgren, Lauri Kuoppamäki, Hedvig Gebhard, Ellinor Ivalo, Rafael Blomstedt, Hilding Ekelund and Arttu Brummer-Korvenkontio.

Uusi Suomi 12.12.1924, p.4, "Piirustuskilpailu". *Kotiliesi* 1925/5, pp. 101—102, Rafael Blomstedt: "Pienkodin sisustamiskysymyksiä".

84. *Käsiteollisuus* 1925/2, p.35, Arttu Brummer-Korvenkontio: "Pienkodin huonekalut".

85. This revolving bookcase was made in Finland in the 1910's at least by the Billnäs company. V. I. Lenin's study bookcase is in the Kremlin Museum in Moscow, August Strindberg's in the Nordiska Museet in Stockholm.

Katalog över Billnäs kontorsmöbler — Luettelo Billnäsin konttorihuonekaluista 1916, Helsinki 1920, p.24. *Arkkitehti* 1929/12, p.193, S. F.: "Kuvia eräästä helsinkiläisestä yksityisasunnosta".

86. *Svenska slöjdföreningens årsbok*, Stockholm 1926, p.21, Axel L. Romdahl: "Konsthantverket i Stockholms konserthus".

87. Aino and Alvar were married in Helsinki on 6.10.1924 by Pastor Toivo Valtari, Aino's brother-in-law.

Keskisuomalainen 5.10.1924, p.3, "Pikku-uutisia".

88. *Jyväskylän työväentalo, tupaantuliaisiin 12. —13.9.1925*, Jyväskylä 1925, p.31, Toivo Lehto: "Jyväskylän työväenyhdistyksen oman kodin historiikkia". See also Note 78.

89. *Jyväskylän työväenyhdistys v. 1925*, Jyväskylä 1926, pp. 3, 8. *Muuramen tuolitehtaan Osakeyhtiö, kuvasto n:o 6*, Jyväskylä 1919, pp. 11, 20. Photograph K 225:6320; Central Finland Museum, Jyväskylä.

90. *Uusi Aura* 21.10.1928, p.6, X: "Nykyajan arkkitehtuuri ja kodin sisustus".

91. Professor Gustaf Nyström, who taught the third and fourth years courses in architecture at the STKK, was absent on sick leave during the autumn term of 1917 and died on 31.12. of the same year; he had thus been Aino's teacher but not Alvar's, though the latter made reference to "my old academic professor Gustaf Nyström".

Suomen teknillinen korkeakoulu, vuosikertomus korkeakoulun toiminnasta, lukuvuosi 1917—1918, Helsinki 1918, p.11.   *Iltalehti* 14.12. 1921, p.4, Alvar Aalto: "Vanhat ja uudet kirkkomme".

92. As far as is known furniture design was not touched on in the curriculum, yet it was possible to work in a furniture factory for the practice required for the Degree in Architecture; apparently both Aino and Alvar did just this.

Interview with Prof. Hilding Ekelund, 26.9.1982.   Interview with Hanna-Maija Alanen (née Aalto), 17.8.1982.

93. The library of the University of Technology was almost completely destroyed in an air raid on 6.2.1944, but fortunately the printed acquisition lists are available, on the basis of which it is possible to reconstruct the situation for instance at the time that Aino and Alvar were students.

Suomen teknillisen korkeakoulun kirjastoluettelo 1911, Helsinki 1911. *Lisäluettelo 1912—1914,* Helsinki 1914.   *Lisäluettelo 1915—1917,* Helsinki 1918.   *Lisäluettelo 1918—1920,* Helsinki 1920.   *Lisäluettelo 1921—1923,* Helsinki 1924.   *Lisäluettelo 1924—1928,* Helsinki 1930.

94. See Note 15.

95. The library of the Suomen Taideteollisuusyhdistys (Finnish Society of Crafts and Design) was in the Ateneum and it forms the framework of the present library of the University of Industrial Arts.

96. See Note 93.   The interest of architects in the history of interior art is indicated by the fact that the copy of *Wohnungskultur und Möbel der italienischen Renaissance* now in the library of the Museum of Finnish Architecture was originally Lasse Björk's (1892—1961), bought by him in 1921, and *Möbel und Raumkunst in England 1660—1800* and *Der Stil Louis XVI* Oiva Kallio's (1884—1964), purchased in 1919 and 1922.

97. Of the books dealing with Gustavian interior art, one of the first was the rather short *Gustaviansk stil i Nordiska Museet* (1926), a broader study was Ernst Fischer's *Svenska möbler i bild* (1931), but the standard work on the subject did not appear until Sigurd Wallin's *Nordiska Museets möbler från svenska herremanshem III* (1935).

98. See Note 93.   This deliberate or unintentional "censorship" by no means prevented the younger generation from getting to know these books, whenever necessary they could buy them for themselves.

99. See Note 93.   The first edition of Alexander Koch's series of books was published at the beginning of the 1910's, so it mainly offered late Jugend interiors; in the second and completely revised edition (neue Folge) the main emphasis was already on Classicistic styles. The volumes in my own library, *Schlafzimmer* (1919) and *Herrenzimmer* (1921), have originally belonged to the architect Matti Finell (1889—1978).

100. According to his own account Alvar in the summer of 1920 had "made a 3½-month study tour of the scandinavian countries at his own expense"; at the beginning he was in Stockholm paying special attention to the construction of the Town Hall, but most of the time he seems to have been in Gothenburg working in the "Ares" bureau which was planning the buildings for the town's Tri-Centennial Exhibition. The following spring he applied in vain for a F. Sjöström Stipend to "study the architecture of South Germany and the Hansa period" (in all probability he meant North Germany), but ultimately received a grant from the State Commission for Architecture to "make a study of the decorative arts in the Baltic countries". This journey took place in late summer and was to Tallinn, Tartu and Riga. His second journey to Gothenburg Alvar made at the end of the summer of 1923.

A. Aalto's stipend application, "Tekniska Högskolan i Finland inkomna expeditioner 1921", n:o 21/148 Sd 1921; HTKK Archives.   *Iltalehti* 12.11.1921, p.3, Alvar A-o: "Miten kaupungintaloa rakennetaan".   *Uusi Suomi* 15.5.1921, p.7, "Valtion arkkitehtuurilautakunta".   *Hufvudstadsbladet* 22.9.1921, p.8, Karl Tiander: "Finländska konstutställningen i Riga".   *Keskisuomalainen* 2.8.1923, p.3, Alvar Aalto: "Suomen kaupungit Göteporissa".

101. *Aitta* 1926/1, p.66, Alvar Aalto: "Porraskiveltä arkihuoneeseen".

102. The altar candelabrum for the Toivakka church designed by Alvar was displayed at the Finnish Society of Crafts and Design's Exhibition in 1925.

Suomen Taideteollisuusyhdistyksen 50-vuotisjuhlanäyttely, luettelo, Helsinki 1925, p.5.

103. Paavo Tynell (1890—1973) was the director and chief designer of Oy Taito. It was in his smithy that all the lamps and church objects designed by Alvar during the 1920's were made.   See also Note 78.

104. Sten Branzell (1893—1959) had met Alvar back in 1918 when a volunteer on the White side in the Finnish Civil War. Branzell was a designer in the Kosta glass factory in 1922—1930; at the Svenska slöjdföreningen's famous Small Home Exhibition in 1917 he had displayed a bedroom suite.

Interview with the architect Markus Visanti, 3.3.1980.   Anne Marie Herlitz-Gezelius: *Vackra ting och bruksting från 10- och 20-tal,* Stockholm 1974, pp.31, 79.   *Arkitektur* 1917/11, p.152, L. I. Wahlman: "Svenska slöjdföreningens utställning af inredningar för smålägenheter 1917".

105. *Käsiteollisuus* 1922/2, p.20, Alvar Aalto: "Oma talo. Miksi sen täytyy olla kaunis".

106. Alvar lived at this address, Vapaudenkatu 53, from the end of November 1923 until February 1924 when he became the tenant of Toivo and Hjördis Forsblom at Kauppakatu 19. After their marriage and honeymoon, Aino and Alvar moved to Seminaarinkatu 18 at the end of October 1924 and stayed there until October 1927 when they left for Turku. These changes in address are best followed in the Jyväskylä newspapers where Alvar ran a permanent advertisement, sometimes in all local party papers: the Social Democrat *Työn Voima,* Agrarian *Saarijärven Paavo,* Conservative *Sisä-Suomi* and Progressive *Keskisuomalainen.*

Interview with Mrs Hjördis Voutila (Forsblom), 16.8.1978.

107. *Sisä-Suomi* 3.12.1933 B, p.2, Eino Auer: "Syntyihän siitä sanomalehti, muistelmia Sisä-Suomen kapalovuodelta".

108. The spiritual and economic isolation of Finland caused by the First World War and the Civil War continued well into the 1920's.

Svenska slöjdföreningens tidskrift 1924, p.61, Gustaf Strengell: "Svenska slöjdföreningens utställning av svenskt konsthandverk och konstindustri i Helsingfors 1924".

109. See Note 17.

110. For example, *Käsiteollisuus* 1925/2, p.34, Arttu Brummer-Korvenkontio: "Pienkodin huonekalut" and *Suomen koristetaiteilijain liitto Ornamo, vuosikirja II,* Porvoo 1927, p.15, Arttu Brummer: "Kodin taiteellisesta huolittelusta".

111. The fanciful leg structure in the table model that appeared in Aino's first sketches for the bedroom suite for Erkki Peräinen and for the ladies' clubroom of the Häme Students' Society, may have been influenced by the French Art Deco.

Drawings; Aalto archives.

112. Yrjö Lindegren (1900—1952) received 3rd prize in the "Living room furniture for a family of small means" competition organized by the Finnish Society of Crafts and Design in 1925. Erik Bryggman (1891—1955) received 3rd prize in the competition organized by N. Boman's furniture company in Turku in 1922; his finest "Light Classicistic" work is, however, the Pompeian type couch for the Turku Seurahuone restaurant.

Käsiteollisuus 1925/2, p.32.   *Arkkitehti* 1922/3, pp.44—45, "Kilpailutuloksia".

113. This time span is most applicable to Finland where Jugend had so totally dominated the preceding period. In Sweden, and especially in Denmark, Jugend had been but a marginal phenomenon, so in these countries there was no such perceptible break between the Classicism of the late 19th century and that of the 1920's as in Finland.

114. *Arkitektur* 1920/12, p.157, L. I. Wahlman: "Rumskonsten på 'Verkstadens' utställning".

115. See Note 90.

Some of the obvious gaps in the information contained in this article are to be explained by the fact that I have never had the opportunity of visiting Aalto's home in Riihitie, Helsinki, or, not counting the drawing archives, of acquainting myself with Aalto's library, photo collection, correspondence or other such sources. To avoid misunderstandings I should also like to point out that all data on Aalto and quotations from his writings have been taken from the original source material found by myself in 1977—81 and not from the later publications on Aalto which are also based on the same material.

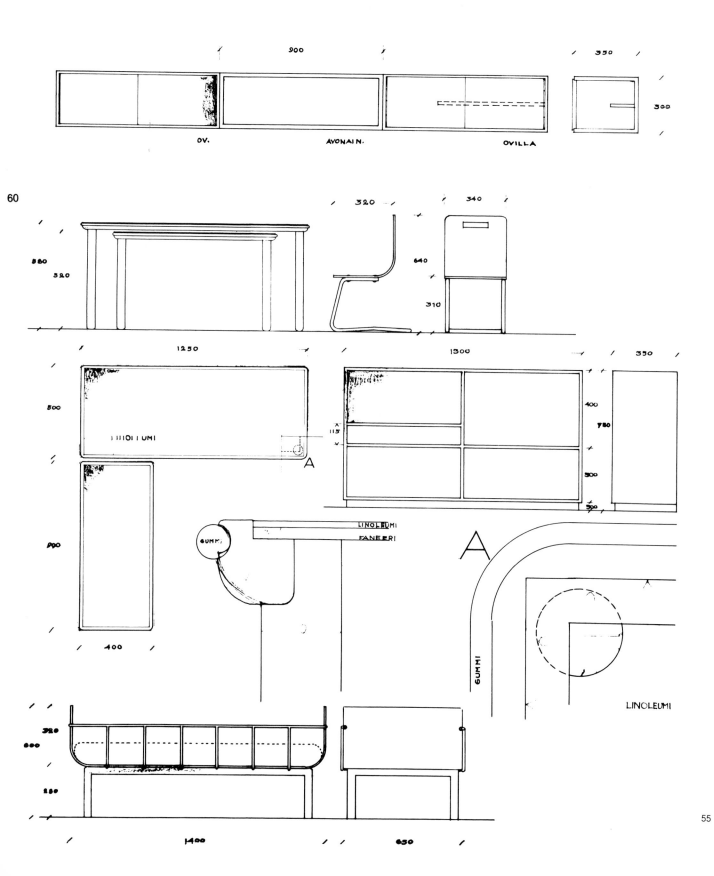

900

350

300

OV.

AVONAIN.

OVILLA

60

320

340

580

320

640

310

1250

1300

350

500

LINOLEUMI

115

400

780

A

500

500

500

400

GUMMI

LINOLEUMI
FANEERI

A

GUMMI

LINOLEUMI

320

600

150

1400

650

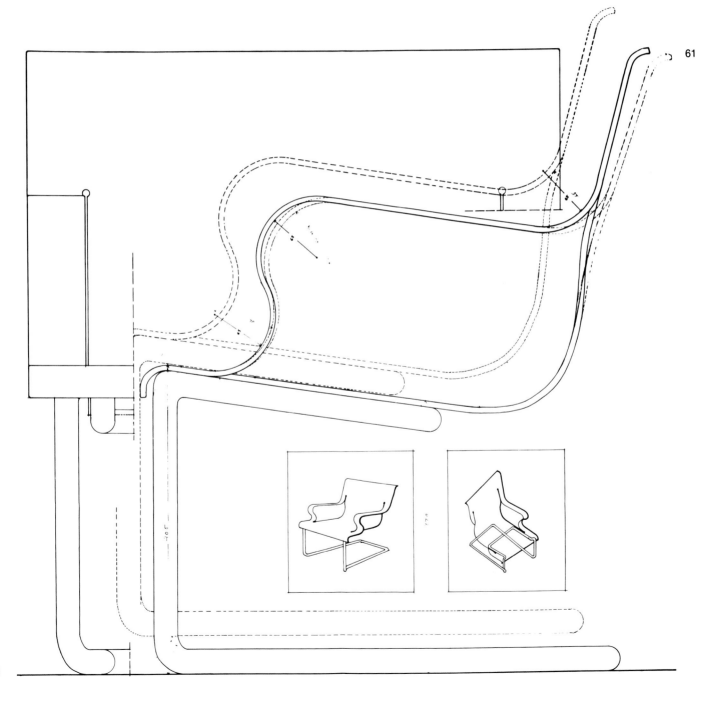

61

56

THE DECISIVE YEARS

Göran Schildt

57   58

59

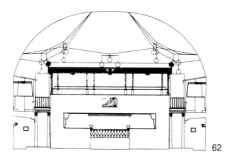

60   61

62

A book about Alvar Aalto's furniture cannot be limited to a description of shapes, an investigation into the technical means of production, or a chronological presentation. It must also include the people who devised and produced the furniture, those who helped launch it abroad, and those who judged and bought it. The ideas, the ideological and practical expectations these people harbored were just as significant for the creation of this furniture as its roots in the styles of the past. It is the human side, in a broad sense, the biographical part of the history of Aalto's furniture which I hope to be able to elucidate somewhat on the following pages.

Aalto's interest in furniture designing had its roots in his ambition to create a uniform and new total environment, which social reformist architects had cherished ever since the days of Ruskin. They were dissatisfied not only with the often arbitrary mixtures of styles which characterized interiors, but above all with the way of life, and indeed with the social conditions, associated with these interiors. When Morris furnished his Red House in 1859, he gave concrete form, through furniture, textiles, and wallpaper, to a less alienated way of life than that which industrialized civilization had produced: a society characterized by handicrafts, a medieval guild spirit, and ardent contact with nature. He was a social reformer, even if his message had little chance of reaching beyond a privileged and relatively limited circle.

The English Arts and Crafts Movement was, as we know, widespread, and also influenced the Finnish architects who were Aalto's teachers and predecessors. Armas Lindgren and Usko Nyström devoted considerable attention to furnishings as part of their efforts to create a Finnish version of the general Art Nouveau movement. Finnish Art Nouveau, or Jugend, as the movement is known in Finland, was strongly oriented towards social reform and in those days was indeed utopian, since it expressed a vision of an independent nation with a harmonious society, rooted in its own traditions and with a culture which an amazed world could not but admire. When Akseli Gallen-Kallela and Eliel Saarinen furnished their homes, they incorporated this whole program into their designs.

Alvar Aalto, who started his architectural career shortly after his country had gained its independence, repudiated the narrow Finnish element in the National Romanticists' vision, just as he broke away from their architectural idiom. Instead, he sided with the Neo-Classicism which was oriented towards Italy and reached Finland from Sweden. The man who provided him with his most important inspiration at the beginning of his career, Gunnar Asplund, was an adherent of this style. But Aalto was faithful to the idea that an architect should serve as a reformer. He made an effort to construct and furnish buildings so that a person who entered his creations would be transformed into a Renaissance man. He saw his home town, Jyväskylä, as a new Florence, with inhabitants who would be just as self-confident, ruggedly individualistic, infatuated with life, and artistically creative as Benvenuto Cellini, the Medicis, and their countrymen.

Aalto designed many kinds of furniture during his Neo-Classical period, mostly for relatives and friends, but also for public premises, as Igor Herler showed in the preceding essay. The thing which was especially characteristic of this early Aalto furniture was its unrestrained freedom in comparison with its predecessors and established styles. This was due to Aalto's mannerism, or provincialism. Just as he admired the old Finnish carpenters who "translated" the forms of Continental Baroque churches into the original wooden constructions of village churches in the 18th and 19th centuries, he himself varied forms in Renaissance and Empire furniture in a consciously audacious way. The goal was, after all, not to imitate the external forms of the past, but to revive their spirit.

Several circumstances were responsible for awakening Aalto from this historical, romantic dream in almost a single day in 1927 and transforming him into a Functionalist. The rationalistic reform movement which had started in the 1920s on the Continent differed from the utopia of Ruskin and his disciples in its attitude towards industrialization. Instead of rejecting machines as the Arts and Crafts Movement did and dreaming of a return to handicrafts, the Functionalists accepted machines, not only as a necessity, but also as a welcome means of reaching such goals as general material well-being, social equality, and the spread of the blessings of culture to all. The new forms of architecture and interior design which the prophet Le Corbusier, the social reformers within the German Bauhaus, and the more theoretical members of the Dutch De Stijl group put forth were certainly rooted in technical practical reasoning, but they had above all a symbolic value as an expression of the new dream of reform. It was not difficult for Aalto to join them. Thanks to the liberal environment in which he grew up and his admiration for his maternal grandfather Hugo Hamilkar Hackstedt, he had a positive basic attitude to technical inventions, machines, and industrial progress. Throughout his whole life he remembered his grandfather's mathematical gifts, pedagogical work, and above all his mechanical inventions for sewing machines, weapons, bicycles, and steam engines. His civil servant father, in turn, passed on to him a paternalistic sense of responsibility for

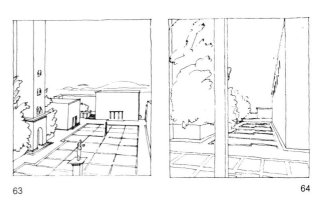

63   64

65

66

67

Fig. 64

68

69 *In 1930 Aalto designed a very modern stage setting for the Turku Theatre.*

70, 71 *Drawings by Aalto made after his first flight in 1920.*

72 *Paimio Sanatorium, site plan, 1929—32.*

73 *Turun Sanomat newspaper building, 1928.*

74 *Courtyard elevation of Aalto's standard apartment house in Turku, 1927.*

64 society's less fortunate, which was strengthened by a more conscious feeling for the people in his wife Aino. Aalto's fascination with the blessings of modern times manifested itself in the middle of the 1920s as a lively interest in airplanes, cars, tennis, and movies. Only a few external impulses were necessary in 1927 to carry him away completely.

Aalto's "conversion" was not an isolated case in Scandinavian architectural circles. Sven Markelius had visited the Bauhaus and the Weissenhof exhibition in Stuttgart in the summer of 1927. He expressed his enthusiasm to Aalto that same autumn. Aalto's colleague Erik Bryggman made a similar trip the following summer, when Gunnar Asplund also became a Functionalist. In 1929, Aalto and Markelius were asked to be members of the newly founded Congrès Internationaux d'Architecture Moderne (CIAM), whose most influential members included Le Corbusier, Walter Gropius, and its secretary Sigfried Giedion.

Aalto's reaction to the new challenge came like a flash. In the autumn of 1927, he designed a "standard apartment house" in Turku which met the new goals fairly well as far as construction, design, and social attitudes went. The

Turun Sanomat newspaper building, designed in 1928, was totally Functionalist, although unindependent in its imitation of Le Corbusier. But when Aalto won a competition for a sanatorium in Paimio in 1929, he did so with a project which was so independent and mature that it was soon recognized as one of the most prominent international creations of rationalistic architecture. The explanation for this exceptionally rapid liberation is that Aalto refused to adopt ready-made solutions. He did not attribute any decisive authority to rationalism's masters on the Continent. He considered himself fully capable of drawing the correct conclusions from the basic premises of the new doctrine.

We can follow the same development in his furniture design, where a limited scale actually permitted him freer experimentation than is possible in expensive and unwieldy building. Aalto's break with Neo-Classicism was reflected stylistically in the furniture designs he made in 1928 for the sacristy of Muurame church and for various rooms in the Lounais-Suomen Maalaistentalo Oy building (the Agricultural Co-operative building) in Turku, including the theater salon, banking facilities, and Itämeri (Baltic) Restaurant. In each case, designs were sent to various carpentry firms for bids. One of them, the Huonekalu- ja Rakennustyötehdas Oy, was outbid for the first two projects, but produced the

69

70

ALVAR 21. 71

furniture for the Itämeri Restaurant. This is how the first contacts — later to be so significant — were made between Aalto and the company's technical director Otto Korhonen.

The Huonekalu- ja Rakennustyötehdas Oy was a well-established and high-quality company which had made furniture before the war for both Russian customers and the respected furnishing firm Boman in Helsinki. Otto Korhonen was a highly experienced professional who had inherited a strong feeling for technically expedient means and esthetically simple forms from the rustic milieu in which he grew up. He was also keenly aware of the new demands made on a company like his by industrialization, mass production, and modern marketing. It was necessary to move away from handicraftsmanship but still cling firmly to high quality. He himself was responsible for technical innovations. For example, he placed the seat of an ordinary chair on top of legs extending to the sides so that the chair could be stacked. Aalto, who was keen on innovations, was impressed and helped Korhonen improve the chair's design. And so their first joint creation, a stackable chair for which Korhonen obtained the Finnish patent, was born in 1929 (even though it was later found that three other inventors in England had come up with the same idea earlier), while it

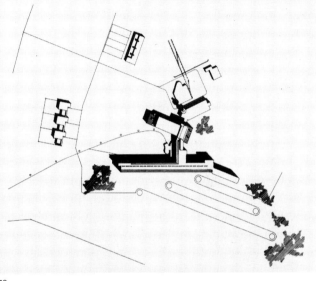

72

73

74

75 Wooden stackable chair, patented by Otto Korhonen in 1929.

76 Chair for the sacristy of Muurame church, 1928.

77, 78 Furniture for the banking department in the Agricultural
Co-operative building in Turku, 1928.

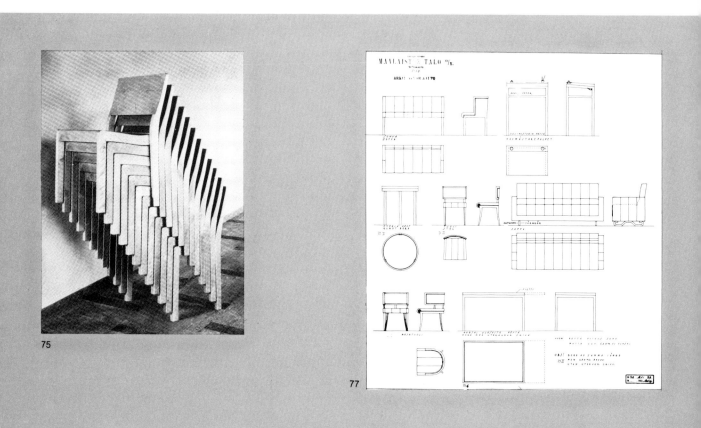

75

77

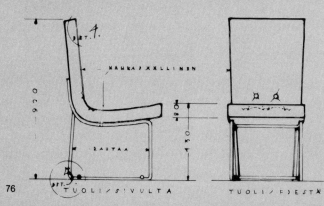

76

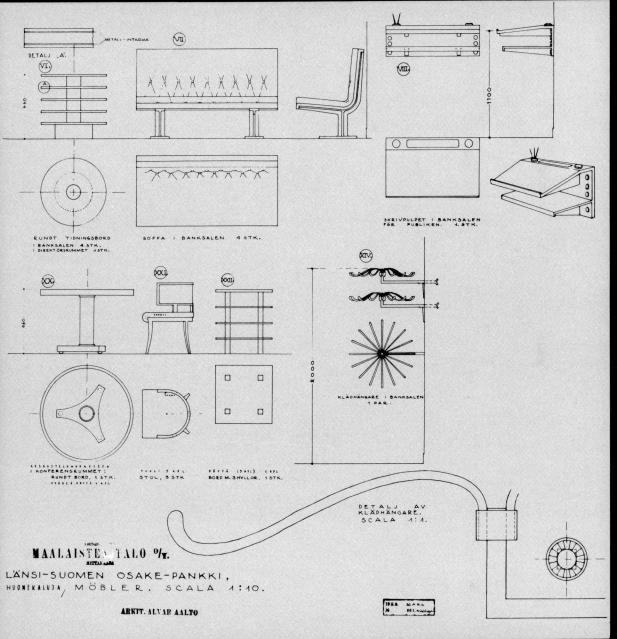

DETALJ "A."
METALL-INTARSIA
VI.
A
VII.

RUNDT TIDNINGSBORD
I BANKSALEN 4 STK.
I DIREKTÖRSRUMMET 1 STK.

SOFFA I BANKSALEN 4 STK.

VIII.

SKRIVPULPET I BANKSALEN
FÖR PUBLIKEN. 4 STK.

XX.
XXI.
XXII.

XIV.

KLÄDHÄNGARE I BANKSALEN
1 PAR.

KESKUSTELUHUONEESSA
I KONFERENSRUMMET:
RUNDT BORD, 1 STK.
PYÖREÄ PÖYTÄ 1 KPL

TUOLI 3 KPL
STOL, 3 STK.

PÖYTÄ (3 HYL) 1 KPL
BORD M. 3 HYLLOR, 1 STK.

DETALJ AV
KLÄDHÄNGARE.
SCALA 1:1.

MAALAISTEN TALO O/Y.
LOUNAS- MITTAKAAVA

LÄNSI-SUOMEN OSAKE-PANKKI,
HUONEKALUJA/ MÖBLER. SCALA 1:10.

ARKIT. ALVAR AALTO

1928 MARS

78

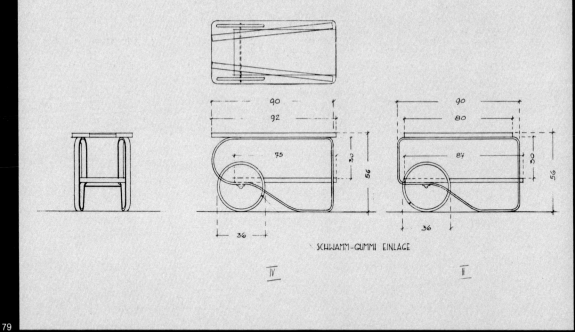

SCHWAMM-GUMMI EINLAGE

IV   II

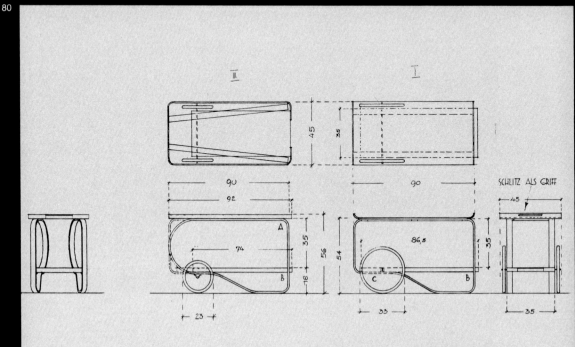

III   I

SCHLITZ ALS GRIFF

I. ACHSE UNABHÄNGIGER VON DEN BÜGELN

79, 80 *Drawings for the tea trolley, around 1936.*

81 *Marcel Breuer's cantilever chair, purchased by Aalto in 1928.*

82 *Marcel Breuer's "Wassily" chairs from 1925 and "Bio" table from 1927 in Alvar Aalto's living room in Turku.*

83 *Advertising pylons by Aalto and Erik Bryggman at the Turku Exhibition in 1929.*

84 *Aalto's "bedroom furniture" at the Turku Exhibition in 1929 containing the chair associated with E. G. Asplund's "Senna" of 1924.*

was, and still is, sold under Aalto's name. This chair was ready just in time to become the main piece of furniture in the auditorium of the Civil Guards' House in Jyväskylä.

In December 1928, a cargo of furniture, ordered by Aalto arrived in Turku from Thonet-Mundus Konzern in Berlin. It consisted of Marcel Breuer's later famous "Wassily" chair, the same designer's cantilevered simple chair, and "Ablegetische" tables. Aalto put some of this furniture in his own home, while he used other pieces to complete the furnishings which he had designed for the Itämeri Restaurant. It should be pointed out that when Aalto spoke of these pieces in interviews and articles, he always called them *"Thonet standard furniture."* It is possible that he was not aware of or interested in the designer's name, since the important thing for him was that the furniture was industrially mass-produced and inexpensive, which made it socially acceptable. The concept standard furniture, like standard house, had been coined by the Bauhaus circle and often appears in Gropius' remarks. Aalto took the idea seriously and remained faithful to it in his own furniture designs.

It did not take long for Aalto to come up with an answer to Breuer's furniture. In the summer of 1929, Turku celebrated its 7th Centenary with an exhibition whose architectural setting, designed by Aalto and Erik Bryggman, anticipated the Stockholm Exhibition's famous festival of Functionalism. The Turku Exhibition also included a furniture pavilion, where the Huonekalu- ja Rakennustyötehdas had its own stand. Thanks to a number of recently discovered photographs of this pavilion and a few letters from Aalto in late summer 1929, in which he described his furniture, we can now form a fairly clear conception of this phase in his work with furniture, and also of the external impulses and his own ideas from which his well-known models from the '30s originated.

According to an article in *Uusi Aura*, June 16, 1929, the main attraction at the Huonekalu- ja Rakennustyötehdas' stand was *"bedroom furniture by architects Aino and Alvar Aalto"* (picture 84) which represented *"a first attempt in the direction of new objectivity,"* since in producing it they had used *"a whole new work method, technically evolved for this project,"* which had made it *"possible to achieve a very high level of standardization."* This description actually fits only the chair in the bedroom suite, since the accompanying cubistic tables, beds, and clothes closet were made of completely normally joined pieces of wood. The chair, however, had a seat and back of molded plywood in one single bent piece, which at least from the factory's point of view had come into being through *"a whole new work method."*

81

82

83

84

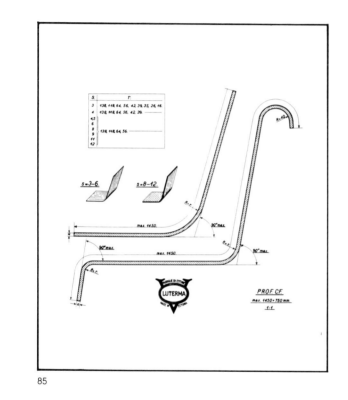

85

86

Actually, Michael Thonet had, as early as 1836, made furniture using a method of molding thin layers of wood, and the Estonian company Luterma had, since the beginning of the 20th century, as the American architecture historian P. D. Pearson has pointed out, specialized in making seats and backs of plywood, used in railroad cars, waiting rooms, and other public premises. The method had also spread to Finland, and there had been used among other things in Jyväskylä in the manufacture of plywood suitcases (picture 86). Korhonen certainly was very familiar with the technique of fixing plywood in set shapes by letting thin layers of wood which had been warmed up and joined with glue cool down in iron presses with various forms. He had evidently recommended it to Aalto as a suitable way of realizing an aesthetic idea which Aalto had borrowed from his admired elder colleague Gunnar Asplund. At the Paris Exposition in 1925, Asplund had presented a luxury armchair in Egyptian style called "Senna," with seat and back forming a soft curve (picture 87a). "Translating" this simple but expensive product of cabinetmaking, perfect in form, into an inexpensive piece of standard furniture of molded plywood must have appeared to Aalto as a logical application of the technical and social program dictated by the new architectural philosophy. Aalto's "Folk Senna" makes a fairly Spartan impression in its uncovered version, but when necessary it could be upholstered with a detachable padded cover, decidedly improving the appearance.

Unfortunately, no photographs have been preserved of another chair which was also featured at the exhibition in Turku and which Aalto mentioned in a letter from the time: a "Senna" which, instead of the conventional wooden legs in picture 87b, had a springy tubular frame borrowed from Breuer's steel tubular furniture as a base for the molded back and seat. This chair, which Aalto, with his ability to coin good slogans, called *"the world's first soft wooden chair,"* was in other words the prototype for what I consider it proper to call the "hybrid" chair (picture 89), since it unites the "soft" elements borrowed from Breuer with the "hard" parts used by Asplund and Aalto. The hybrid chair was improved quite quickly by adding a bend on the bottom part of the tubular steel frame; Aalto was granted a patent for this innovation, which made the chair stackable.

Aalto most probably showed yet another type of chair at the Turku Exhibition which had a certain Art Nouveau touch (picture 90) but was stackable, thanks to its ingenious construction. It was made by the Huonekalu- ja Rakennustyötehdas at least until 1932 and was found at the Milan Triennial as late as 1933.

85 *Molded plywood seats in the Luterma Catalog for 1931.*

86 *Plywood suitcases manufactured in Jyväskylä in the 1920s.*

87a *Erik Gunnar Asplund's "Senna" chair, 1924.*

87b *Aalto's "Folk Senna," 1929.*

88 *Aalto's "Folk Senna" with non-springy tubular metal legs and a round table with metal base and nickel-plated metal shelves in Aalto's apartment in Turku, around 1930.*

89 *Stackable "hybrid" chair, 1930 (Wohnbedarf Catalog).*

90 *Aalto's stackable chair with Art Nouveau touch, 1929.*

87 a

87 b

88

89

90

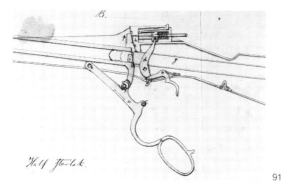

91 *Hugo Hamilkar Hackstedt's repeating rifle with ergonomic shape.*

92 *Stackable chair (Thonet competition, 1929).*

93 *Chair for two sitting positions (Thonet competition, 1929).*

94 *Chair resembling "Senna" design (Thonet competition, 1929).*

95 *Cantilever chair (Thonet competition, 1929).*

96 *Serving table (Thonet competition, 1929).*

97 *Nest of tables (Thonet competition, 1929).*

The realization that Aalto probably borrowed the soft shape of the seat and back for the hybrid chair from Asplund and that Korhonen initiated him into the secrets of molded plywood naturally says nothing about the artistic intentions which lay behind the new chair. Ideas and impulses of all possible kinds do, after all, continually surround us, while the interesting thing is why we choose certain impulses and close our eyes to others. In Aalto's case, we can say that Breuer's furniture appealed to him to the extent to which it was a standardized industrial product and was built upon the dynamic principle of "springiness," but repelled him to the extent to which it followed geometrical principles of form and used metal, a tactilely unpleasant material.

In the work of Asplund, on the other hand, he once again found the organic forms which he knew from his admired grandfather's inventions, for example his repeating rifle, with an organic, ergonomic form (picture 91), and his strange sewing machine. It is a question of being drawn by temperament to "soft forms," but also of a greater proximity to the world of nature than to that of abstract geometry. The first result of these forces of attraction and repulsion was the hybrid chair, which accepted Breuer's principle of springiness but replaced metal with a more appealing material, wood, when there was contact with the body, at the same time as the overall shape was an affirmation of the feeling for organic forms of Aalto's grandfather. Aalto's style in furniture, like his style in architecture, was in other words characterized by a view of what human functions a designer should take into account that was different from the ones schematic Functionalism took note of. The English critic P. Morton Shand said as early as 1933 in a radio lecture (published in *The Listener*, November 15) that Aalto *"has left the bare bones of doctrinaire functionalism behind him."* He did this in 1929, when he created his hybrid chair with plywood seat and back.

We can follow the next step in Aalto's thinking in furniture design in the six entries he submitted on September 9, 1929, to Thonet-Mundus in Berlin, which had announced a large international competition for new models for its tradition-steeped company. Thonet had a particularly close relationship to the new architecture right from the start. Le Corbusier liked to furnish his experimental buildings with Thonet chairs and Aalto did the same with his newly completed standard apartment house in 1929, when he organized a little exhibition in the form of a furnished apartment with ideal standard furniture to show how a modern home should be equipped. Thonet's openness to the new architecture can be seen in the fact that it included Pierre Jeanneret (Le Corbusier's brother), Josef Frank, and Gerrit

T. Rietveld in the furniture competition jury. Aalto's entry comprised a simple chair which could be stacked according to the Korhonen principle (picture 92), an armchair with two different sitting positions ("Arbeit-Ruhe") (picture 93), a four-legged chair with the upper part in the same style as that of the hybrid chair (it had a similar removable padded cover for additional comfort) (picture 94), and finally, a highly attractive solution on paper to a problem which had begun to occupy Aalto: to "translate" Breuer's springy tubular base into wood (picture 95). In his entry, Aalto connected three curved front legs, one after the other, with the foremost smoothly merging into the seat and back. Two other entries which were later to mature into actual models were also included in Aalto's competition material: a smaller "Ablegetisch" (serving table), which was designed like a sled, with runners (picture 96), and a larger nest of tables, ten of which could be placed one under the next without the difference in height being more than 9 centimeters in all (picture 97).

Aalto did not win any prize in the Thonet competition, and his drawings were returned. The reason was not only that there were over 4000 projects for the jury to consider, but also that Aalto's entries were technically unsatisfactory. The failure certainly taught Aalto that he would have to continue and intensify his work together with Korhonen. The Thonet competition, like the classical Thonet furniture, was based on the use of round rods of beech as a material. It is strong and can be bent in all directions, while birch, the cheapest and most easily obtainable material for furniture in Finland, is strong, but otherwise has completely different characteristics. Beech was imported to Finland, and the Huonekalu- ja Rakennustyötehdas had it, too, but in order to produce the inexpensive standard furniture Aalto and Korhonen wanted, it was necessary to concentrate on birch. It has often been said that wood was closer to Aalto both emotionally and esthetically than cold metal tubing, but we must not forget the economic factors which also contributed to the creation and success of Aalto's furniture. Wood is Finland's most important raw material. It is in the national interest to export it in a highly processed form.

The next stage we know of in the development of Aalto's furniture is the Minimum Apartment Exhibition in Helsinki in 1930. Aalto was the exhibition's instigator, organizer, and chief architect, but Erik Bryggman, P. E. Blomstedt, and Werner West also had their own sections. Aalto had imported the idea direct from Germany, where a considerably larger exhibition organized in the same manner had been shown in Munich in 1928, and where Aalto had had the

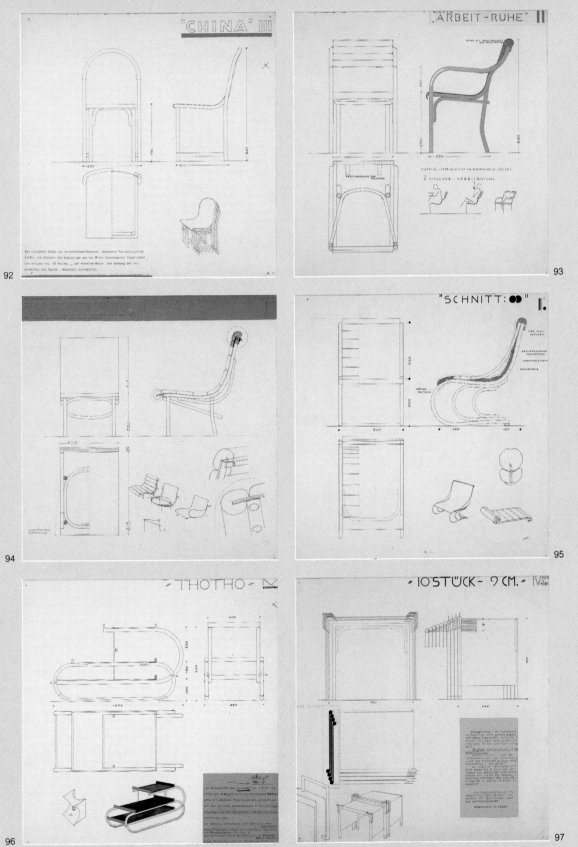

98

rücken und sitz sind in jede beliebige
lage verstellbar.

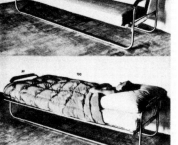

63 modell aalto ⬭ pat.
bettsofa
durch einen handgriff wird dieses be-
queme sofa in ein bett verwandelt.

99

opportunity to study the exhibition "Die Wohnung für das Existenzminimum" in Frankfurt am Main in 1929 at the CIAM meeting. The minimum apartment (i.e. the smallest possible dwelling produced and furnished most economically which also satisfies all reasonable requirements for a good standard of living) was the ideal test field which a whole phalanx of young, reform-minded architects needed in order to break down obsolete conventions surrounding living and to define the design of a modern home. One of the main goals was industrially mass-produced, inexpensive, but practical, well-made, beautiful furniture. Aalto's work with furniture that year concentrated on this program. At the exhibition, he furnished his dwelling with stacking chairs in Art Nouveau and hybrid styles, with his first models for standard lamps, and with a sofa which, with a single pull, could be transformed into a wide bed (picture 99). This convertible sofa and the stacking hybrid chairs, both of which were only found in the form of untested models, were sent by Aalto in the beginning of 1931 to his friend Sigfried Giedion in Zürich. Giedion had recently started up the companies Palag and Wohnbedarf AG in the spirit of the new CIAM movement.

This takes us back to Aalto's participation in the second CIAM meeting in Frankfurt in 1929. There he had made important personal contacts with leading figures in international architecture. Most of his new friends also came to the Stockholm Exhibition the following summer. In Stockholm, he formed an even faster friendship above all with Sigfried Giedion, Walter Gropius, Laszlo Moholy-Nagy, and the English critic P. Morton Shand, all of whom were to play important roles in Aalto's development.

Giedion immediately welcomed Aalto to his company and especially took to both the hybrid chair and the convertible sofa. The former, with the springy tubular base which made it stackable, was hailed by Giedion as *"das Ei des Columbus für Stahlstuhl in Restaurant, Bar, Kaffé"* (the Columbus egg of tubular chairs for restaurants, bars, cafés). It was made lighter and more elegant under Giedion's supervision before serial production was begun (picture 89). The plywood seat was imported from the Huonekalu- ja Rakennustyötehdas in Finland, while the base was made in Switzerland. It could be upholstered with a removable, padded cover when necessary. From 1932, the hybrid chair was also made by DESTA (Deutsche Stahlmöbel) in Berlin, which, however, soon relinquished production to Thonet-Mundus. The convertible sofa was also modified under Giedion's supervision and was ready for production in the spring of 1932, when Wohnbedarf displayed its Aalto furniture at an exhibition in Stuttgart. Wohnbedarf remained

100

101

102

both a manufacturer and a retailer of imported Aalto furniture, which explains why the whole Swiss pavilion at the World Exposition in Brussels in 1935 was furnished with Aalto furniture, whereas the Finnish pavilion only presented a few Aalto chairs.

It is probable that Moholy-Nagy mediated the Bauhaus school's method of ascertaining the plasticity and range of expression of various materials through handicraft experiments in the form of abstract works of art. In any case, Aalto and Korhonen began in 1930 to saw, bend, split, stretch, join, and glue laminated wood in all possible ways in order to find new forms for furniture. The first tangible fruit of this work was an armchair version of the hybrid chair, with the armrest made from the same piece of plywood as the seat and back (picture 101). The next step was to use birch, instead of Thonet's easily bent beech, for the bearing frames. This was done by gluing 3-mm thick layers of bent birch slats together into an elegant, rounded side frame to which the seat could be fastened. Here Aalto gave the method of molding plywood a new function, using it to form the thin bearing frame. This is how the "Paimio armchair," with its seat and back of springy plywood fixed on a closed frame was born (picture 103). It was a way of making a wooden chair "soft" for which Aalto sought a patent.

The Paimio Sanatorium was completed in December 1932, but since it takes a fairly long time before a new type of furniture comes into production after it has been designed, the furniture in this building mostly shows the stage which Aalto had reached at the end of 1931. There were only a few test chairs with wooden spring arms together with a few initial attempts to utilize wooden legs bent at a right angle. A stacking round stool with a tubular base, in accordance with a variation of Aalto's patent for tubular chairs, had, however, been given its final form (picture 102) as had a stackable armchair in a more constructivist vein (picture 100).

The idea of opening the Paimio chair's closed frame so that it could be given a springiness similar to that of tubular chairs was simple to formulate, but difficult to implement technically. The open curves in wood showed a tendency to change shape when the material dried out or when the springiness relaxed after the chairs had been used for a while. It took some time for Korhonen to surmount these difficulties. The first satisfactory results were reached when the tubular base of a child's chair (picture 105) was "translated" into a base of laminated wood (picture 106). The "adult" chair with a springy base of wood was shown for the

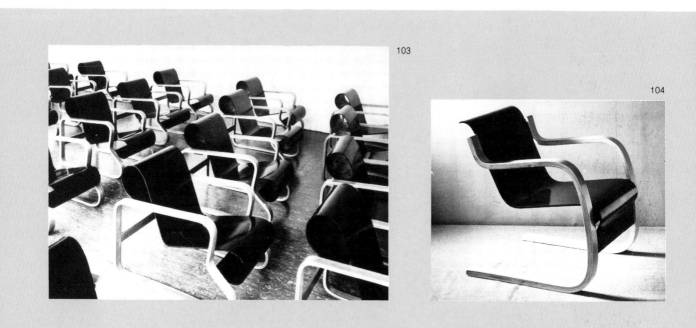

103

104

105

106

107

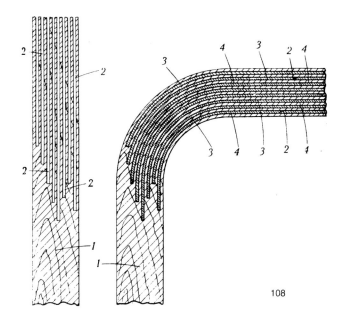

108

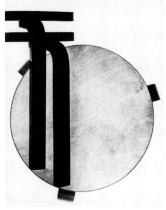

109

110

first time at the Nordic building fair in Helsinki in the summer 1932, but production could not begin in earnest until the end of the year (picture 107).

Aalto's most important discovery in furniture design, in his own estimation, was the idea of the "bent knee." A piece of solid birch wood was sawn open at the end in the direction of the fibers, and thin pieces of wood were glued into the grooves. The wood was then bent to the desired angle, in this case 90°. He obtained a patent for the method in Finland and abroad, with the exception of Germany, where this method was not accorded any special position among the well-known ways of bending laminated wood. Aalto never obtained any full patent protection for his technical innovations in furniture, and he was plagiarized even more often as far as designs were concerned. Plagiarization of this kind done by no less a personage than Marcel Breuer must have given him the feeling that Breuer was taking revenge for Aalto's design loan from him a few years before. Uncertain patent protection in furniture design resulted in Aalto himself being threatened by Thonet with litigations over the wooden chairs with spring arms.

1933 marked Aalto's big breakthrough as an internationally recognized furniture designer. Both of his important innovations, the wooden chair with spring arms, and the angled wooden leg, were shown and aroused great interest at the Milan Triennial in 1933. The most famous of the CIAM meetings took place in Athens in August of the same year. Aalto attended it, accompanied by a young Finnish follower, art critic Nils Gustav Hahl, who was actively involved in the new ideas and was accepted as a CIAM member without his being an architect. In Athens, Aalto reinforced his friendship with the talkative, hyperintelligent, epicurian English critic P. Morton Shand, who also took a kindly interest in Hahl. None of these three gentlemen was to realize the significance of this meeting until two years later. But at this time, P. Morton Shand promised to organize an exhibition of Aalto's furniture in London that very autumn.

The job of arranging an exhibition was not easy. Aalto had a marked inclination to forget agreements. The Huonekalu-ja Rakennustyötehdas was unable to write letters in English, and the furniture which was to be sent to London was delayed week after week. Nonetheless, the exhibition was opened on November 13, 1933, under the egis of *The Architectural Review* (its chief critic being P. Morton Shand). The place was the "snob department store" Fortnum and Mason's in Piccadilly, and Aalto himself was responsible for the sophisticated exhibition arrangements. One important ingredient was *"laboratory wooden objects,"* experimental

111-115 *Laboratory experiments with laminated wood: approximate datings, Fig. 111 1931, 112 1931, 113 1937, 114 1955 and 115 1955. (Photographs taken from multiples produced by the Alvar Aalto Foundation in 1979.)*

112

111

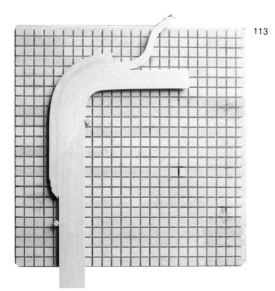

113

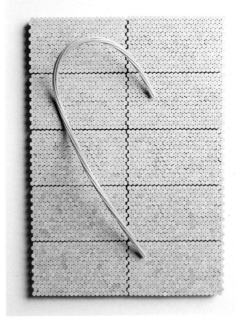

116 *Four chairs and ways of sitting. Illustration in the catalog of Aalto's exhibition at the Museum of Modern Art in New York in 1938.*

117, 118 *Sketches from the 1940s.*

80

reliefs made in Korhonen's workshop as an impetus to furniture design. The whole thing was presented as an *"exhibition of ideas,"* and as an alternative to the extravagant tubular furniture Londoners had been offered as exponents of the modern style. *"Aren't we all tired of modern things which are expensive because they are modern, modern because they are snob and snob because they are expensive,"* wrote the managing director of *The Architectural Review*, H. de C. Hastings, in his presentation. The English reacted with amazing positiveness to the inexpensive and elegant Aalto furniture. The demand for it was so great that P. Morton Shand and some of his friends started up a company, Finmar, to import Aalto furniture. Its sales snowballed during the following years, and it also sold furniture to the U.S.A. and Australia, while companies in France, Spain, Belgium, and Italy — in addition to those already established in Switzerland and Sweden — began to sell as much Aalto furniture as the Huonekalu- ja Rakennustyötehdas was ever able to produce, to the accompaniment of enthusiastic articles in innumerable architectural journals.

The modest factory and its cautious owner, who did not know how lasting demand would be, were not the only reasons for the delay in getting Aalto furniture. Even more problematic was Aalto, who never answered letters. Clients, above all Finmar and Wohnbedarf (which in March 1934 repeated the Fortnum and Mason's exhibition in Zürich), considered it unheard of and incomprehensible that anyone could be so bohemian and indifferent to economic realities as Aalto was. Both companies threatened (in vain) to cut off all ties with him. Actually, the bohemian attitude was Aalto's means of self-protection, his only way of dedicating himself to creative work despite external pressures instead of being turned into a frustrated, mercenary soul. When the chaos culminated in the summer of 1935, and Finmar was swamped with calls from disappointed cus-

tomers, while Aalto calmly made himself unavailable on a fishing trip to Lapland, the sorely tried P. Morton Shand chanced to think about Aalto's follower in Athens, Nils Gustav Hahl. He was poor, conscientious, and culturally well informed, which made him ideal for the job of "rescuing angel."

Hahl was responsible for the Finnish pavilion at the World Exposition in Brussels that summer. He corresponded with young Maire Gullichsen, daughter of a prominent industrial family, who painted in her free time and had also begun to collect works of art. She and her husband, industrialist Harry Gullichsen, were Hahl's good friends and put the greatest trust in him as an art expert and guide to the radical social ideology to which they felt drawn in a way unusual in their circle. The correspondence between Hahl and Maire Gullichsen gives us highly interesting glimpses into events which were also to become important for Aalto. The two had for some time planned to start some kind of avant-garde art gallery in Helsinki. When, in late summer 1935, Hahl unexpectedly found himself the Huonekalu- ja Rakennustyötehdas' correspondent, with the job of bringing some order to Aalto's furniture business — at the instigation of P. Morton Shand — he drew a logical conclusion. He introduced Aalto to Maire Gullichsen and proposed that the three start up a company which would partly serve as a "Palag—Esprit Nouveau center" in Helsinki, i.e. be a sales and propaganda center for the new housing ideology with Aalto furniture as its specialty, and partly exhibit modern art. The division of labor among the participants was clear: Aalto was to be the creative force, Hahl the executive, and Maire Gullichsen the financier and propagandist. Maire Gullichsen remembers that she was very shy and uncertain at her first meeting with the already famous architect. *"But he looked at my legs, found them pretty, and said O.K."*

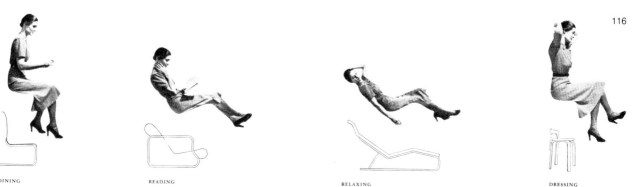

116

DINING   READING   RELAXING   DRESSING

Artek started operations in an office in December 1935, and opened its store at Fabianinkatu 31 in Helsinki on March 1, 1936, under the leadership of Nils Gustav Hahl. Aino Aalto was naturally in on the enterprise right from the beginning, which gave the company two bosses, not a completely successful arrangement. In spite of difficulties, periodical plans to transfer furniture production from the Huonekalu- ja Rakennustyötehdas to a factory owned by the company, and a decision to make the art sector independent as Galerie Artek, the company developed and carried out its job magnificently, thanks to Aalto's growing international reputation and the great demand for his furniture and interior furnishings. Nils Gustav Hahl was killed in the war in 1941; Aino Aalto then headed the company until her death in 1949. Since 1954, Artek has been run from the Rautatalo, an office building designed by Aalto, at Keskuskatu 3 in Helsinki with Åke Tjeder as its successful director since 1957.

Most of the Aalto furniture has been made by Otto Korhonen's old company the Huonekalu- ja Rakennustyötehdas Oy in Turku. Today the company has grown into a large and very modern factory complex with an annual production of over 100,000 pieces of Aalto furniture. But Aalto furniture has, as mentioned, also been made in Germany and Switzerland (mostly tubular models). In the 1930s, Kolho Oy made certain models when the factory in Turku was running at full capacity. In the U.S.A., Aalto furniture was produced by Eggers in Wisconsin beginning in 1940, and sales were handled by Artek-Pascoe in New York. Right after the war, when the run-down Turku factory could not be enlarged, Aalto started Svenska Artek with a Swedish businessman, Ernst Sundh. Its factory was located in Hedemora and produced furniture from 1946 to 1957.

The "heroic period" of Aalto's furniture actually ended in 1933, and thus spanned only five years during which Aalto's fundamental ideas took shape. Developments did not, however, stop then, even if longer periods passed between radical new projects. Right up to the war, there were three ideas which mainly gave Aalto furniture a new content. There was the construction of a triangular console, which was intended to support wall shelves and clothes racks, but could also be used to fasten small tables to the wall and as an umbrella stand (pictures 121 and 122). There were two versions of a tea trolley (pictures 123 and 124), which were further developments of the "serving sled" submitted to the Thonet competition in 1929. And there was the original method of making tables and chairs out of loose planks which were held together with steel wire. I am referring to the garden furniture designed in 1939 for Villa Mairea (picture 125).

119

120

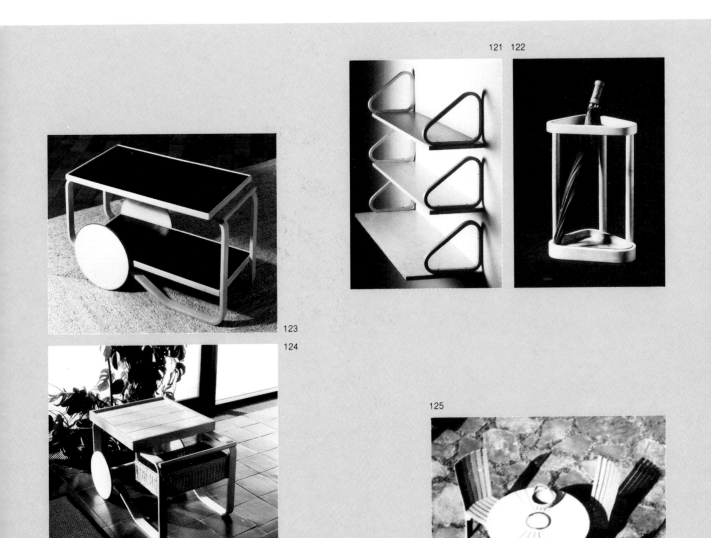

121 122

123

124

125

126

127

130

129

128

126 *"Bent knee" leg, 1933.*

127 *Two sided Y leg, 1947.*

128 *Fan-shaped X leg, 1954.*

129 *Socket leg, 1956.*

130 *Split bend used for a stool, 1947.*

131 *National Pensions Institute, Helsinki 1956. Interior.*

132 *Maison Louis Carré, Bazoches, France 1959. Interior.*

133 *Chair designed by Maija Heikinheimo in the Aalto spirit.*

134 *Chair designed by Aino Aalto in the Aalto spirit.*

135 *Aalto's chair for the H55 Exhibition in Helsingborg, 1955.*

136 *A chair with the spaghetti-like construction designed for the National Pensions Institute in 1956.*

137 *The most produced Aalto stool — more than a million in 50 years.*

Aalto called a furniture leg *"the column's little sister,"* because by discovering new leg constructions, he changed the style of his furniture just as clearly as the Doric, Ionic, and Corinthian columns each resulted in a special order, or style of architecture. The simple corner-bent leg was joined in 1947 by the Y leg, which in 1954 was followed by the fan-shaped X leg. A fourth "order," a leg made out of spaghetti-like wooden strings, which appears in certain furniture from 1956 for the National Pensions Institute in Helsinki and for Maison Louis Carré in France, proved less suitable for further development.

The triumphal procession of Aalto furniture was backed up by unique external circumstances in addition to the supporting power of constructive ideas and formal beauty. First of all, capable helpers all the way from Otto Korhonen and the assistants at Aalto's office, to a staff of highly qualified furniture designers at Artek — most of all Aino Aalto and Maija Heikinheimo — worked out variations on Aalto's fruitful basic ideas under his supervision and experimented their way to the best final result: technically, economically feasible models which truly satisfy public needs. Certain models, like the round stool with three or four legs, have become just as common in Finland as the Thonet chair was in its day. When Aalto and Korhonen got their first model ready in 1932, and were throwing it around the factory floor to test its durability, Aalto exclaimed, *"This stool is going to be made in the thousands!"* Not even in his optimistic enthusiasm could he dream that fifty years later, far more than a million of these stools would exist. Other projects remained one-of-a-kind models, like the elegant armchair made for the H55 Exhibition in Helsingborg (picture 135).

131

132

133

134

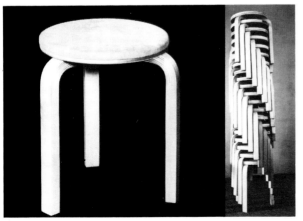
137

135

136

138

138 *Herbert Bayer's cover for the Wohnbedarf Catalog, Zürich 1933.*

139 *Exhibition of Aalto's furniture at Fortnum and Mason's, London 1933.*

140, 141 *Aalto furniture in the Finnish Section at the Milan Triennial, 1936.*

142, 143 *Aalto furniture in the Finnish Pavilion at the Paris World Fair, 1937.*

144 *Exhibition of Alvar Aalto at the Museum of Modern Art, New York 1938.*

Other external circumstances which had been decisive for the creation and spread of Aalto's furniture were the exhibitions and new buildings which gave him the impulses and framework to work out new furniture applications. We have already mentioned Turku's 7th Centenary celebrations in 1929, and the accompanying furniture exhibition, the Minimum Apartment Exhibition in 1930, and the London exhibition in 1933. A number of showings in the 1930s which were important for Aalto should also be mentioned, because of their importance for his growing world reputation. The Milan Triennial in 1936, with a large Aalto section, and above all the major Aalto exhibition arranged by the Museum of Modern Art in New York in 1938 which definitively established Aalto's international standing. At these showings it was possible to see his creations in the original, while his buildings, in spite of the lovely pictures in architectural journals, remained elusive, in far-off Finland. In Sweden, Aalto solidified his reputation by taking part, as an invited guest, in the exhibition arranged by Svenska Slöjdföreningen (now called Svensk Form, the Swedish Society of Crafts and Design) at Liljevalchs' in 1934. In Norway, Aalto furniture was shown by Norsk Brukskunst (the Norwegian Society of Arts and Crafts) in 1938, and in Denmark at the "Spring Exhibition" the same year. After the war, there were innumerable exhibitions, handled more indirectly through Artek. But as late as 1954, when Aalto was supposed to have an exhibition at the NK department store in Stockholm, he found it embarrassing not to present any new ideas. So he introduced his furniture with the X leg for the first time, saying that he had gotten the idea from a young lady's pleated skirt.

Certain buildings should be mentioned as having given Aalto the impulse to devise new types of furniture. We have already referred to the Paimio Sanatorium. The Viipuri town library has perhaps been associated too closely with the advent of the first corner-bent furniture legs, but it is in any case the milieu for which he created the most important applications of this idea. For Villa Mairea, Aalto would certainly have designed more than just sofas, armchairs, and garden furniture if the war had not intervened. The post-war buildings which should be mentioned as especially important in this connection are the National Pensions Institute and Maison Louis Carré. A certain shift in interest from furniture to lighting fixtures could be noted during the '50s and '60s, possibly because work with furniture had earlier reached useful results, while the selection of lamps had long been limited.

139

140   141

In conclusion, we can say that Aalto's work with furniture was not a sideline to his architectural work; it was of central importance for his buildings, too. The move from steel tubes to bent wood and the "laboratory experiments" with wood which Aalto carried out in order to create furniture gave him vital impulses as he sought and found his own architectonic style in the 1930s. This was completely clear to Gustaf Strengell, when he wrote in an article in 1933: *"A look at the furniture exhibited here* (at the London exhibition) *will show that Aalto has developed a new and specially architectonic idiom, and has not only found a new special method of producing furniture"* (*Uusi Suomi*, November 12, 1933).

This idiom does not embrace the barren utopia of rationalism. It expresses a striving towards a biological duet between man and nature which is one main element in Aalto's artistic message: a new program of reform for humanism aimed at letting us survive harmoniously on this earth.

SOURCES

The sources for this study are — unless otherwise stated — the letters, drawings, photographs, annotations, and printed matter in the Aalto Archives, Munkkiniemi.

144

142

143

145 *Drawing for the Paimio armchairs 41 and 31, 1931—32.*
146, 147 *Alternative conceptions for the Paimio armchair 41, 1931—32.*

88

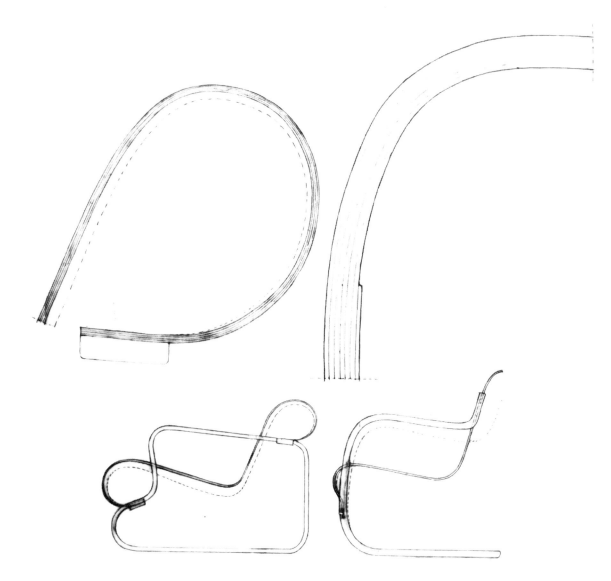

145

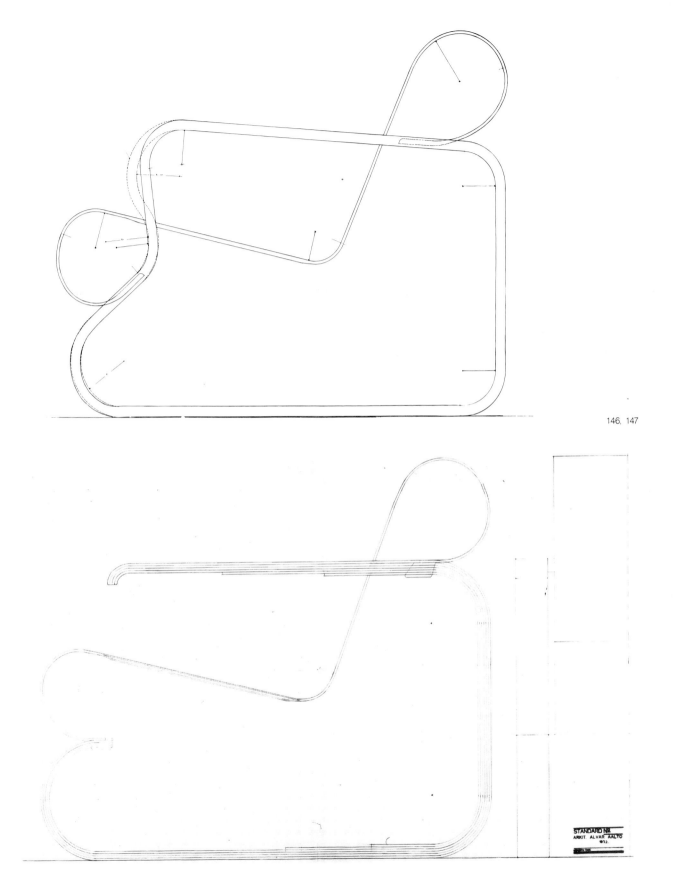

146, 147

STANDARD No.
ARKIT. ALVAR AALTO
1932.

WORKSHOP RECOLLECTIONS

Marja-Liisa Parko

90

In the 1950's it was the custom at Artek to clear the drawing boards when anticipating a visit by Alvar Aalto. The artistic director, Maija Heikinheimo, was responsible for keeping order and she apparently knew of the maestro's delight with the sight of clean, white paper. This only occurred to me after reading extracts from an advance copy of Göran Schildt's biography of Aalto, *Valkoinen pöytä* (The White Table). Whatever the real reason be, Maija Heikinheimo's attentiveness was an expression of the reverence shown the maestro at Artek in those days.

I have worked in this atmosphere and my views derive from my time at Artek. These recollections are based on my own experiences and interviews with colleagues and fellow workers concerning the customs that have prevailed in the Helsinki drawing office and the Turku furniture factory.[1]

When Artek was established in 1935 it did so with a ready-made series of furniture models. Further models were designed for the collection as required by the interior projects undertaken — furniture for hospitals, offices, libraries and restaurants, and even for maternity clinics and kindergartens in collaboration with the Mannerheim League for the Protection of Children. Objects that did not belong to the standard collection were normally made somewhere else than at the Turku factory. And before long it was found

150

necessary to add soft, upholstered easy chairs and sofas to the lighter, all-wood basic range. In the middle of the 1940's, the designer Erkki Kataja, a second-generation upholsterer, joined the staff of Artek and right up until the end of the 1970's all upholstering on Artek and Alvar Aalto furniture was carried out at his workshop.[2]

When I joined Artek it was not so long after Aino Aalto's time. Indeed, four of the designers there had begun work under her direction. The exacting working traditions had been carried over by Maija Heikinheimo who, upon succeeding Aino Aalto, became responsible for the development and implementation of all Alvar Aalto's ideas on furniture and interiors. After Maija Heikinheimo's death in 1963 the design work on Alvar Aalto's interiors was transferred from Artek to his own office. Thus collaboration as it had been came to an end.

AMA

In the literature on Alvar Aalto, his wife, Aino Marsio-Aalto, is remembered as an unassuming and serious-minded woman and a similar impression is held by her contemporaries at Artek. Aino Aalto was a calm, motherly figure, professionally responsible and socially conscious, yet still a strict superior. When discussing a problem, it was typical of her to say to the assistant designer, *"Let's think about it."* And at Artek they would add, *"Let's think about it — up to our elbows."*

Aino Aalto would place a folio of drawings before the novice to illustrate the working methods of the office, the choice of materials available, the scales used, technique of expression and texting. The custom continued under Maija Heikinheimo. The first job was to copy drawings from the archives. Though the original initials were retained, the drawing was re-dated. In this way nearly all of Artek's archives of original drawings, complete with their dates, were destroyed. In the second half of the 1940's with the new, second generation of Aalto furniture ready, Maija Heikinheimo drew, in her beautiful hand, the complete standard folio anew and re-dated all the drawings.

Any attempt to define the relative shares of Aino and Alvar Aalto in design work has been considered difficult, if not impossible. Using Artek's own drawing archives it is, however, easy to see how those works in Aino Aalto's name and initialled *"AMA"* differ from those of Alvar Aalto and signed *"AA"*. Aino Aalto's work displays a confidence in both style and proportion, but is cautious in nature, even commonplace. Those designs with Alvar Aalto's initials made

151

152

153

154

155 *Maija Heikinheimo stepped into the shining world of Alvar Aalto and threw herself into the work of collaboration. A photograph from the 20th Anniversary Exhibition of Artek in 1955.*

156 *Armchair from Maija Heikinheimo's first period with Artek. Only a few pieces were made in 1939.*

92

155

156

during Aino Aalto's lifetime are, on the other hand, audacious and experimental.

Being more of a match for her husband than his other collaborators, Aino Marsio-Aalto made independent adaptations and variations of Alvar Aalto's themes being able to grasp their essence as if they had been her own.

MHHO AND AA

Maija Heikinheimo came to Artek in 1937 after having met Alvar Aalto at the Paris World Exhibition. Prior to that she had been the first permanent designer at the Asko Furniture Factory in Lahti. There she had designed, for example, for Asko's new steam bending machine, an armchair[3] that I would consider an Aalto variant. Later on Maija Heikinheimo viewed this kind of copying quite differently and condemned the following of fashion as the easy way out.

During the war years Maija Heikinheimo was with the Wilh. Schauman Oy company in Jyväskylä. In 1945 Aino Aalto persuaded her to return to Artek who then needed someone with experience in the furniture industry and in organizing exhibitions.

The war years were followed by a period of creative enthusiasm. Maija Heikinheimo appears to have played a major role in the development of the Aalto's new series of furniture. She was also entrusted with the job of liaison with Korhonen's factory.

Hardly any of Alvar Aalto's original sketches have survived at Artek. Once the final drawings were ready all notes and drafts were destroyed. In Maija Heikinheimo's folio for autumn 1946 there are, however, Aalto's sketches for the Y bend and chair No. 612.

The idea of bending legs in two directions had occupied Alvar Aalto back in·the 1930's. The principle of it can be seen in an early wood relief. The Y leg came to be produced at the Svenska Artek Hedemora factory and was first shown to the public at the "Konstruktiv form" (Constructive Form) exhibition in Stockholm in 1947.

During the years 1946—48 some 23 models, inclusive of variants, were designed. Eleven of these were actually new types and included the light wooden armchair No. 45 which is the best selling item of today's Aalto furniture. It is this chair that is particularly linked to Maija Heikinheimo at the Turku factory: *"Maija knows best what Aalto furniture should look like."*

93

It was under her management that Maija Heikinheimo developed a drawing initialling system intended to delude. She used her own initials, *"MHho"*, only for objects of minor value. The most important works in her life were for the interiors of buildings designed by Alvar Aalto 1949—63, yet I have never seen her name listed as one of his collaborators. Although Maija Heikinheimo was fully aware of her own worth, for some reason or other she concealed herself behind a veil of anonymity.

Maija Heikinheimo often worked late into the night. In correcting the drawings of her staff she marked on the Artek's stamp: *"Designed by AA"*.

The following case is quite typical. Huge easy chairs were to be designed for Louis Carré's drawing room. Hellevi Ojanen drew them at Artek and Maija Heikinheimo discussed them with Alvar Aalto at his Munkkiniemi office. Aalto expressed his approval and Maija Heikinheimo marked the designer as Alvar Aalto. Hellevi Ojanen would have been content enough with the Artek's stamp but did not wish to have the wrong name marked for the designer. Maija Heikinheimo settled the matter by redrawing the chair. Two of them were actually made and in the final version the so-called spaghetti bend was used.

159

160

Maija Heikinheimo was an expert at consulting with Alvar Aalto. As both were hard of hearing, they would sit with their best ears forward. Being highly sensitive and receptive, Maija Heikinheimo was well able to transcribe Alvar Aalto's intentions to us younger people. *"Maija knows without asking what the Professor means"*, they said at Artek.

Even without Maija Heikinheimo's mediation it was easy to discuss with Alvar Aalto. He was considered, with reason, to be ill-mannered but was suggestive and able to inspire confidence. Accordingly, all of us tried to bend to his will. When Alvar Aalto corrected with his soft pencil and shaking hand the original drawings we had made with such an effort, the result brought more the joy of comprehension than disappointment. Aalto also was in the habit of illustrating his advice with perspective sketches of the room on the edge of the furniture drawing.

FROM THE BACK ROOM TO THE FACTORY FLOOR

During the war, Pirkko Stenros attended school in Jyväskylä and stayed with the furniture store owner Parkkonen. He recounted stories of a mad architect couple boiling pieces of wood in a saucepan in the back of his store in the 1920's. This was a perilous thing to do, or so the story goes. So apparently Aino and Alvar Aalto began their researches into bending wood already during their Jyväskylä years.

With the Aaltos' move to Turku in 1927, they found an enthusiastic sympathizer for their experiments in the factory owner Otto Korhonen. He himself had already been trying to bend wood in his factory, the Huonekalu- ja Rakennustyötehdas Oy. What had happened was that Otto Korhonen had acquired a mass of choice beech from the Kylliäinen workshop when this company, for whom he was guarantor, went bankrupt at the end of the 1920's. Kylliäinen had been steam pressing wooden parts for bicycles. When Alvar Aalto, in his own words, began the struggle *"against metal in furniture design"* he used just the kind of material that Otto Korhonen had acquired by chance: beech battens and beech hoops[4].

The story goes that Marcel Breuer got the idea of bending metal tubes for furniture from the gleaming curves of the bicycle.[5] How paradoxical that in Alvar Aalto's own work the bicycle, too, should have had its own, though now forgotten role. The first springs for the Paimio Sanatorium furniture were pressed from beech. Hundreds of metres of beech battens were used in the interior of the Paimio Sanatorium.

The retired master carpenters, Aarne Virta and Kaarlo

Paasikivi, who had joined the factory in 1926 and 1927 respectively, remember the early efforts. The factory had a lot of aspen, then much used for the frames of furniture. This aspen was of a pure and even quality, unlike the birch which was unsorted stuff brought in by local farmers from their own sawmills. A combination of aspen and birch laminations was first experimented with, but aspen proved unsuitable for bending. Also the birch, being of irregular quality, fractured easily.

There were frequent failures in experiments with the Aalto leg. The bend fractured when curved grooves were sawn on the concave face of the bend. It weakened when the wood was sawn open down grain and shrunk on drying. In the 1940's the same error was repeated in the Hedemora factory in Sweden when producing the Y series, even though the carpenters were on loan from Korhonen. Only photographs remain of the elegant but over-thin bends. Success only came when staggered longitudinal saw cuts were made in the part to be bent which were then strengthened with glue-covered plywood insert.

Another problem was the gluing of damp wood. Casein glue, being slow drying and highly resistant to water, ultimately proved to be the best and is still used today in the factory for cold bending. During the war this glue was unavailable as its basic raw material, milk, was rationed. During the worst years of shortage, 1943—44, Aalto legs were replaced by straight ones fixed to the top by combed joints.

In actual fact, it was like going back more than a decade. The Huonekalu- ja Rakennustyötehdas' own collection included Katri Waren-Waris' designed round table with shelves, the so-called W table. Its legs were also fixed with combed joints in a series of crosses. With the commencement of collaboration between the Korhonen factory and the Aaltos, this table was simply changed to one with Aalto legs.

In the early days there was a stack of Aalto's three-legged stools on display in the window of the Turku factory shop. As the stools dried, they were impossible to separate from each other. The carpenters remember the work of almost half a century ago: *"The bend was made at exactly the desired angle. Not understanding the nature of wood, it was assumed that the bent wood would either straighten or remain at the right angle when dry."*

As the curve of the Aalto leg does not stay absolutely in place, the bend has to be less than a right angle. The angle corrects itself upon drying, but continues to respond to changes in humidity. This technical inexactitude, however,

161 *Sketch of the war-time Aalto leg.*

162, 163 *Early experiment for the Y bend without plywood insets.*

164, 165 *The Y bend in its later and final form.*

166 *Standardized tower of Babel or the stacking principle.*

161

162   163

164   165

166

96

beautifully illustrates the organic philosophy associated with Alvar Aalto's work.

WORKING CUSTOMS

There was nothing particularly unique about Alvar Aalto's and Otto Korhonen's method of working. It is comparable to a later example of the reciprocal relationship between Aalto and the metal worker Viljo Hirvonen in the design of lamps. Discussions would be illustrated by sketches, often made on bits of cardboard, which would be the basis for Hirvonen's first model. His technically creative contribution often inspired Aalto to further improvements. This mutual inspiration continued until the prototype was ready from which the working drawings were made for the files.

Virta and Paasikivi recalled how Aalto used to hold talks with Korhonen in the "h'office" of the Huonekalu- ja Rakennustyötehdas. Korhonen would then interpret Aalto's ideas to his craftsmen. One model would be made after the other as *"it weren't what was meant"*. The final, approved model would then be drawn on a small scale (1:10) for the files. The object itself, on the other hand, was the working drawing and model for new production series. Even today, the prototype is always on top of each stack in Korhonen's warehouse.

Alvar Aalto visited the factory more infrequently than the women who had also participated in developing furniture, Aino Aalto and Maija Heikinheimo. He would, however, spend days behind the bench designing his wood reliefs, says Jaakko Koskinen, who was himself responsible for making many of Alvar Aalto's bend wood reliefs.

After the war the factory was managed by Otto Korhonen's sons, Paavo and Pekka Korhonen. With the end to rationing, mechanization began. Again, the most difficult problem proved to be the gluing. The use of heat demanded a fast setting glue. It was not until the 1960's that the bending of Aalto legs and the long curves for the armchairs was done mechanically. Using a urea resin glue and a high frequency generator heating press, the bend was pressed into shape in a few minutes. On the other hand, all the long springs and closed curves continued to be made by hand.

At the end of summer 1981 the long springs for easy chair No. 39 were pressed in the Korhonen factory in Littoinen. The work was done in exactly the same way as 40 years before using the combined skill of two carpenters. Air-dried laminates, dampened overnight, were glued, banged square and fixed at the ends. The wood was forced round

167

168

169

170

171

172

173-178 *Bending the armchair curves in 1981.*

179 *The above curves completed.*

180 *Unfinished consoles before being sawn apart.*

173

176

174

177

175

178

a birch form, one man using his whole body to bend the wood as the other clamped on the female parts of the form as the bend progressed. It took about half an hour to press one spring.

After bending the spring is kept in the form for a day and then stacked for drying, held by wedges, at room temperature for at least five weeks. The drying process is checked and the wedges tightened daily.

The enclosed curves are nowadays made at Helle's joinery in Raisio near Turku. The degree of handwork is even greater in the making of the triangular consols. Here Helle and his son fold the cooling bundle of laminates round a small, steel form. The curves are made using a pivoted, long handled steel roller, the most difficult and acutest angle last. The wood is forced under great pressure in order that the screw clamps can be fixed tightly against the seams.

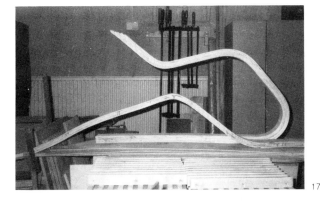
179

Not even the experts are familiar with the production methods used in Aalto's furniture. In 1947, Gotthard Johansson, the Swedish art historian and critic, wrote in the Swedish newspaper *Svenska Dagbladet* a comparison between Alvar Aalto's and Bruno Mathsson's production. In his opinion, Mathsson's furniture was, paradoxical though it may seem, handmade standard furniture, whereas Aalto's, due to its pure simplicity and functional form had been adapted to industrial production.

The degree of mechanization is relative. These days a simple Aalto leg requires some 30 individual operations and the X leg demands almost 50 separate stages.

Alvar Aalto's own words hold true for the Aalto leg: *"Decoration, monumentality, forced adaptability of forms are all things that subtract from an object's possibilities of variation... A standard article should not be a definitive product; it should on the contrary be made so that the form is completed by man himself..."* This is a quotation from a lecture given by Alvar Aalto in 1935 to the Svenska Slöjdföreningen (Swedish Society of Crafts and Design) and quoted in Göran Schildt's book *Luonnoksia* (Sketches). The modest birch wood knee is undoubtedly the most important invention of the collection. It is not a finished object in itself but the brilliantly conceived module with unlimited applications.

180

The later variants of this one-way bend leg are the two-way, constructive Y leg and the decorative, radially fixed X leg. Though representing, perhaps, a richer and more advanced stage in Aalto's design work than the earlier innovation, they are not so versatile in their use in making furniture.

181

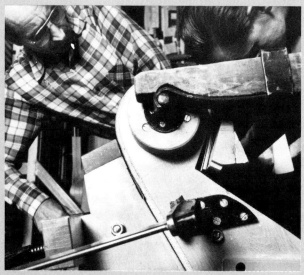

182

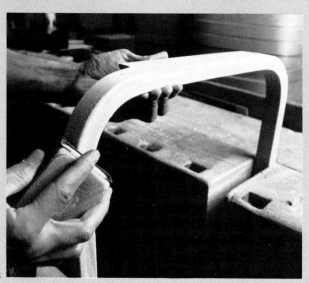

183

184

185

186

100

188-191 *Store of bent pieces for furniture.*

192, 193 *In the busy 'fifties Maija Heikinheimo managed to do other interiors than just Alvar Aalto's. The Imatra library, 1954, an extension to the elementary school (architect Alexis Lindquist).*

194 *Maija Heikinheimo planned innumerable industrial arts and interior exhibitions. Photo of the Artek Exhibition in Stockholm, 1954.*

188

190

189

191

Without going too deeply into technical details, I have below listed the various stages in the production of Aalto legs today (1981):

1. Timber selected from air-dried stock
2. Sawn to measure
3. Edges trimmed
4. Planed
5. Stacked in drying chamber
6. Two pieces glued to make pair
7. Smoothed on belt sander
8. Slots sawn into end to be bent
9. Ends dipped in water
10. Placed briefly in steamer
11. Glue covered plywood pieces placed in slots
12. Plies forced by compressed air to bottom of slots
13. Leg pairs loaded into high frequency generator press
14. Legs about 5 minutes in press form
15. Excess plywood sawn off
16. Legs loaded into drying kiln, left for 4 days
17. Leg pairs sawn down middle
18. Excess of plies on edge removed
19. Machine where both ends sawn to desired length and top planed to make it flush with seat and holes drilled for screws
20. Sides smoothed on wide belt sander
21. Surfaces and edges smoothed on belt sander
22. Final smoothing done by hand
23. Legs cleaned of dust by compressed air
24. First coat of lacquer by individual dipping
25. Fine finishing by hand
26. Cleaned
27. Top coat of lacquer by individual dipping
28. Remove dried blobs of lacquer from feet
29. Legs stored at normal room temperature.

Using this method, some 1000 chair legs and 500 table legs are produced daily in the factory.

CUSTOMER RELATIONS

Artek's interior projects were almost without exception pure Aalto interiors, even when they did not concern one of Alvar Aalto's own buildings. Maija Heikinheimo surprised us all when in planning the now vanished interior for the Finnish Embassy in Vienna, she used Aalto furnishings alongside older furniture. This was one of her last jobs, aesthetic and

192

193

194

cultivated. Side tables with Aalto legs and tops from mahogany had been suggested for the embassy. As these were not on display at Artek's shop in Helsinki, Maija Heikinheimo just took the ambassador and his wife to see a similar table in the nearby Karjakunta butcher's shop. This unceremoniousness was quite unlike Maija Heikinheimo, but in this case she relied on the intelligence of her client and her own proven abilities.

The adaptability of an object for a multitude of purposes is typical of Aalto furniture. This wide scope originates in the functionalist principles behind the design. The furniture is constructed from mass-produced parts and can thus be varied to suit different environments. Even though major projects served Alvar Aalto as a furniture laboratory, the starting point with his furniture has been the modest home and not the luxury building, as he himself has emphasized. Perhaps that is why furniture originally designed for a private villa is equally suitable for a children's home as that for a public building the more intimate setting of the private home.

Artek used furniture in interiors in the way inherited from Aino Aalto, though it is true her simple rationalism acquired certain alien sophistications under Maija Heikinheimo. Artek in the 1960's had already strayed from the principles of the 1930's, partly as a result of Alvar Aalto's own development, partly in an attempt to reach a wider public.

It has taken more than four decades for Artek to win the confidence of the lay public. On the other hand, some of the experts, particularly architects in Finland and especially abroad, had enthusiastically welcomed the collection before Artek was even established.

Following the success at the London exhibition in November 1933, Korhonen's capacity was strained by huge orders from abroad. Yet in the same month a furniture dealer in Oulu complained that: *"Not a single piece has been sold, though people will perhaps appreciate them one day. We are, however, doing our best to market them."* Both the content of the lament and its note of optimism can, on the basis of the company's correspondence, be considered typical of the prevailing attitude in Finland.

Workers in the Huonekalu- ja Rakennustyötehdas were openminded about Aalto's furniture. They had the right to work the material at hand. Whenever a rocking chair or desk chair was required, it would be made by combining pressed seats with legs or a revolving base. The carpenters whom I interviewed do not recall ever having considered Aalto's furniture as strange or unusual.

There were many factors that aroused uncertainty among customers. In line with the European reform movement, Artek's programme included only individual pieces of furniture, yet the general public was reluctant to dispense with suites and ensembles. Neither was the use of natural birch self-evident, its whiteness was considered unfinished. Staining and polishing black remained, therefore, for a long time the more acceptable finishings.

FOR SMALL HOMES OR THE WHOLE WORLD

The nationalist-minded critics who dominated the 1930's looked upon Artek's international ventures with suspicion. In the journal *Ajan Suunta* in 1935, Arttu Brummer could not help but give his unwilling recognition: *"The furniture industry is intimately tied up with social questions and in the end it is they that determine the designers' work. Much has been done in our time to raise the standard of the common people's homes. Possibly Aalto's furniture is an indicator for future furniture designers or possibly we shall develop furniture in a more individual and cosy direction."*

Though Artek gained a strong foothold in the interiors for civic buildings, gaining another one in poorer homes proved more difficult. A draft plan by Nils Gustav Hahl from spring 1941 still exists for the marketing of furniture in the countryside. Through the creation of a retail network, supported by exhibitions and advertisements, it was hoped to widen the range of customers in Finland. Artek, with its internationally representative standard models and collaboration with foreign companies and subsidiaries, was compelled during the war years to concentrate on the home market. Hahl wrote: *"The cosmopolitan intellectualism used hitherto has to be changed into an attitude more exoteric, yet the forms of popularization must be carefully chosen so as not to offend the enlightened part of ordinary public."*

The language used in the countryside advertising campaign tells of a condescending attitude and difficulties in selling furniture considered socially reformist. Even today, it is rare to see Alvar Aalto's furniture in homes in the countryside.

Another defeat in trying to extend the social programme was experienced in 1944. The Finnish Parliament had approved a law making housing loans available for front-line veterans. As public funds were to be used in the purchasing of furniture, it was considered necessary to control both quality and price. This task was entrusted to the Väestöliitto (Family Welfare Association) who arranged a competition among furniture manufacturers on the basis of existing

195, 196 *Artek's first appearance abroad after the outbreak of war was at the "Vi bo i friluftsstaden" Housing Exhibition in Malmö, 1944.*

197 *Despite rationing and raw material shortages the major overseas order for the Seniors' Dormitory at Baker House was fulfilled in 1948. In the foreground the specially reinforced armchairs.*

models. The furniture available for those taking up loans was to be mass-producable, cheap in price, sturdy in construction and functional, yet fulfilling the requirements of good taste and artistic values. They were not to be suites, but individual pieces suitable for the interiors of small homes. The panel of judges included representatives from the Finnish Association of Decorative Artists Ornamo and the Association of Finnish Architects SAFA. One would have imagined that Aalto's furniture would have won a place but when the results were announced 1945 not one of Artek's 36 entries was among the 67 items chosen.

Despite these setbacks, the demand for Aalto furniture from the very beginning has always exceeded production capacity. In the 1930's, Artek furniture was advertised as inexpensive, standard models. During the war, prices were controlled. Now when we have reached the 1980's the same, standard models have acquired an air of expensive exclusivity, perhaps because the original ways of making them and high quality have been preferred to developing production techniques. Even so, nearly all Aalto furniture has undergone changes in materials or technology.

With the end of war the foreign markets reopened. The first major project in the United States was the Baker House student dormitory at M.I.T. New clients brought forth new ideas. Olav Hammarström, the site architect, drew attention to the relaxed life style of American youth. Much concerned, he wrote to Alvar Aalto telling how students frequently sat crosswise when trying to read, start to doze off and then put their feet up. Artek took serious note of this and accordingly fortified the structure of the armchairs.

In practice, the large, complete Aalto interiors have by no means always been preserved. Only a few pieces of the original Paimio Sanatorium furniture now remain. Even the National Pensions Institute in Helsinki has discarded some of its original furnishings. On the other hand, quite surprisingly some early Aalto furniture is still intact in smaller, unchanged interiors such as Wahlman's hat shop in Pohjoisesplanadi in Helsinki.

Attitudes towards Aalto's furniture have ebbed and flowed. Exhibitions have played their role in influencing the public as, too, has Artek's shop. Since the beginning of Aino Aalto's time, the textile designer Sinikka Killinen has been responsible for displaying the furniture. Though the models have over the decades remained the same and always available, from time to time some of them have been taken out of production. The alternating attention paid to Alvar Aalto and his work has been reflected in sales and calls for the reintroduction of earlier models.

105

195

196

197

"THE TEN COMMANDMENTS"

106

Though Artek's objectives have changed, much still remains of its original and ambitious programme. Of all the major founders of the company, Maire Gullichsen is still with it, for she has never at any stage lost her faith in Alvar Aalto.

When the company was founded in 1935, an operations chart was drawn up inspired by Functionalism using slogans borrowed from the 1930 Stockholm Exhibition.[6] It is claimed to have resulted from a dialogue between Alvar Aalto and Nils Gustav Hahl. An enlarged photocopy of the original pasted on board was kept in the Artek drawing office up to the 1970's as a kind of "Ten Commandments".

It depicted the interconnection of modern visual arts, rational furniture production and popular educational work. To further this trinity, a series of radical exhibitions was to be held, a sales organization for Aalto furniture created and critical and propagandist writings were to be published. A complex arrangement of boxes, underlined statements and arrows all led to the slogan printed in block capitals at the bottom of the page: *"FÖR ÖKAD MONDIAL AKTIVI-TET"* (For increased world-wide activity).

No longer is Artek associated with the world of social and aesthetic radicalism. The company has acquired an established reputation. Its very stability has turned it into a national institution.

In a self-assured advertisement in a newspaper in the 1930's a comparison was made between Aalto's furniture and Viennese chairs. How true this implicit faith in victory proved to be, for Artek's furniture collection has indeed enjoyed a long life.

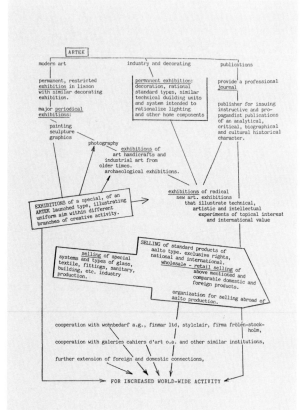

198

REFERENCES

1. I have tried to make do with as few references as possible. My main sources have been: Artek's Archives, Huonekalutehdas Korhonen Oy's Archives and interviews conducted in spring 1981 with the following people: Martti Anttila, Maire Gullichsen, Sinikka Killinen, Paavo Korhonen, Pekka Korhonen, Jaakko Koskinen, Hellevi Ojanen, Kaarlo Paasikivi, Marja Pystynen, Sonja Sandell, Ben af Schultén, Åke Tjeder, Pirkko Vaara-Stenros and Aarne Virta (see detailed list on page 179).

2. The upholsterer Jorma Kuusivaara was responsible for all the upholstery work at the Turku factory.

3. Riitta Miestamo, *Suomalaisen huonekalun muoto ja sisältö* (The Form and Substance of Finnish Furniture), Lahti 1981, pp. 38—40.

4. The birch legs of bar stool No. 64 were not long ago joined with a beech hoop.

5. Christopher Wilk, *Marcel Breuer: Furniture and Interiors*, New York 1981, p. 37. In addition to repeating the well-known story of the bicycle, Wilk also refers to Breuer having experimented with aluminium tubes before opting for tubular steel furniture. The apparent influence which Breuer and the Aaltos had on each other has also interested researchers. And is it just a coincidence that in two photographs of Aino Aalto taken in the thirties she is sitting in the armchairs she was advertising in precisely the same position as the young girl on the cover of Breuer's furniture catalogue a decade before? See Wilk, p. 54 and *Bauhaus Archiv-Museum: Architektur, Design, Malerei, Graphik, Kunstpädagogik; Sammlungs-Katalog*, Berlin West 1981, pp. 158—159.

6. It is, perhaps, an exaggeration to say that the slogans were borrowed. The Stockholm Exhibition did, however, propagate the idea of the interrelationship of interiors and modern art, standard types, rationalization, and internationalism. Compare this, for example with *Acceptera, facsimilutgåva av 1931 års upplaga med efterskrift av Anders Åman*, Arlöv 1980 (Accept, a facsimile edition of the 1931 original with a postscript by Anders Åman).

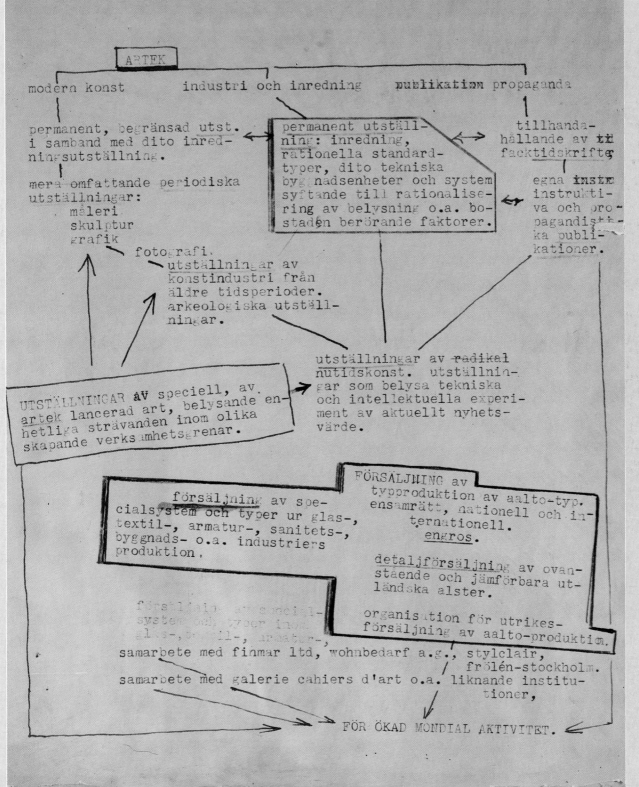

200 *Sketch of various applications of the Y leg, 1946.*

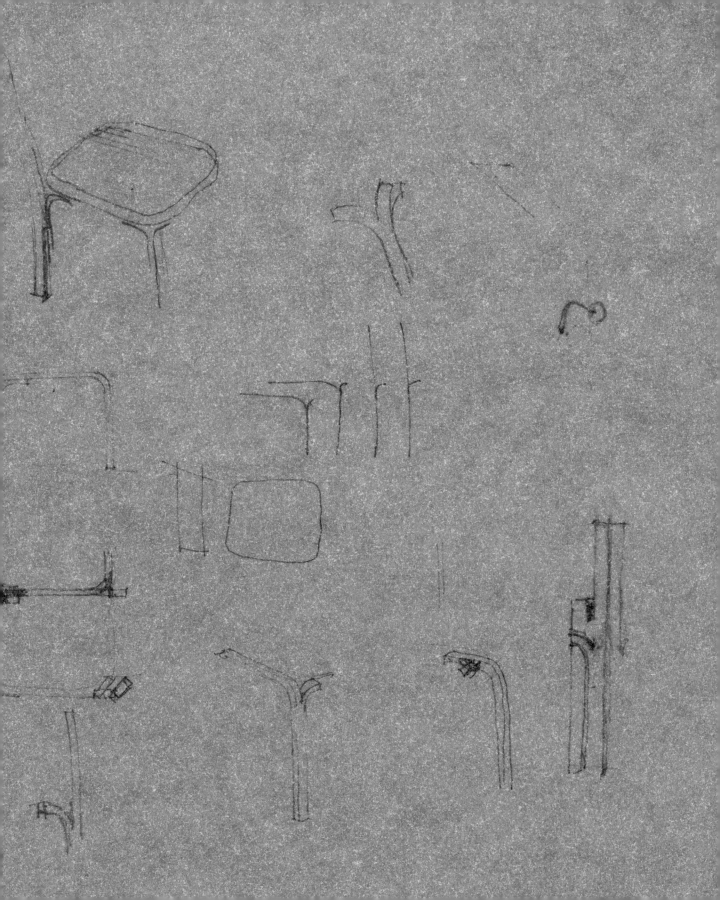

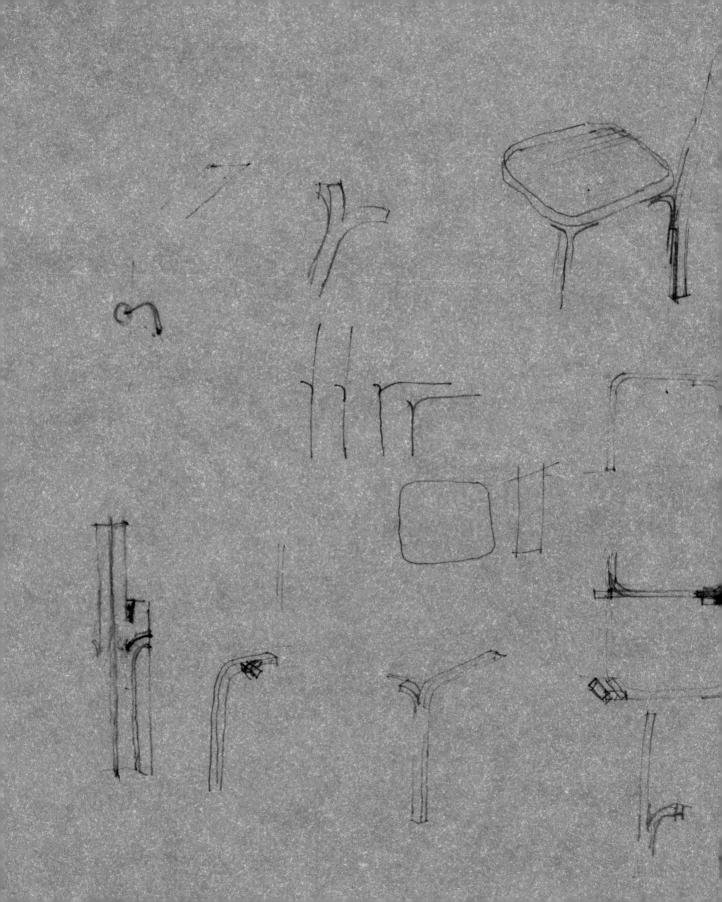

36.   50

48. –70

12. 10 46

EXCERPTS FROM ALVAR AALTO'S ARTICLES ON INTERIOR AND FURNITURE DESIGN

Motorboats, buses, trains, refrigerators, and record players have been juxtaposed with what in times past was regarded as belonging to a higher plane and was called the noble art of interior design. All these new objects now appear with the same pretentions to being taken as cultural artifacts. It means that the design industry's creators are dropping their earlier attitude and stepping down from their assumed height to work in all domains and give form to all articles that are included among life's necessities. I see it as a very positive manifestation that the artist is in a sense denying himself by going outside of his traditional sphere of work, that he is democratizing his production and bringing it out of a narrow circle to a wider public. The artist thus steps in among the people to help create a harmonious existence with the help of his intuitive sensibility, instead of obstinately upholding the conflict between art and nonart which leads to acute tragedies and a hopeless life.

"Stockholmsutställningen" (The Stockholm Exhibition)
Summary of an interview in *Åbo Underrättelser,* May 22, 1930

•

It requires radicalism to avoid creating a superficial comfort and instead to search out the problems whose solution could create the conditions for better architectural work and achieve truly usable criteria for people's well-being in their everyday lives.

"Tukholman näyttely" (The Stockholm Exhibition), *Arkkitehti,* 1930

•

Modern man—and the family—are more mobile than before. This is reflected in furniture's mechanical characteristics.

Sixty square meters—and morning exercise for the whole family: this assumes that the furniture can be easily moved and folded up.

There are large, 200-square-meter apartments where morning exercise becomes almost comically impossible, to say the least, in among heavy cupboards, symmetrically placed tables, undisturbable monumental masses, and diverse fragile decorative glass.

On the other hand, moveable and foldable furniture enlarge a minimal dwelling. And in fact, the whole method of designing the interior that I have mentioned aims at enlarging the dwelling by developing its use possibilities.
. . .

People's predilection to surround themselves with a special world of forms, be it however primitive, has often been brought up in protest against housing construction and interior design of dwellings based on mass production. Question: these dwellings produced for profit which aspire only to present taste, with Empire-style imitations, or the interior decorating business, which does public relations for all types of unusable status furniture, factory baroque, etc., at cheap prices—do they create the perfect conditions for the free individual?

. . .

In this modern society it is possible, at least theoretically, for the father to be a mason, the mother a college professor, the daughter a film star, and the son something still worse. Obviously each would have special needs to be allowed to think and work undisturbed. The modern dwelling must be built in accordance with these needs.

In the same manner, women's emancipation leads to totally new demands on work conditions, such as easy cleaning and consideration of different utensils' weight and mechanical utility.

It is funny to observe how people in general primarily understand form as a fashion phenomenon, an aesthetic sensation; imagine, for example, metal tubing furniture that would actually be weightless and have increased mechanical possibilities. Different designs for chairs which have meant less wear on rugs, etc., have in many cases been treated as purely formal novelties.

"Asuntomme probleemina" (The Dwelling as a Problem), *Domus, 1930*

•

A confrontation with the mass of the neue Sachlichkeit produced in recent times causes a person to take a skeptical attitude and makes him ready to pursue loyally all criticism directed against it. One realizes, of course, that even the true rationalism, which has been created during the last ten years, may be lacking in many ways and often precisely vis-à-vis the concept of humanity, but the question is how "free-form" formalism will become the savior. Modern industrial design is a fairly good answer to this question. Modernism has, of course, essentially made its breakthrough not on its own but on rationalism's authority. Modernism has run amuck with the world of forms that has arisen through the analysis of materials, new working methods, new social conditions, etc., and made of it a pleasant compote of chromed tubes, glass tops, cubistic forms, and astounding color combinations.

. . .

We have conceded and we should be agreed upon the fact that objects that properly can be given the label rational often suffer from a noticeable lack of human qualities. If we disregard for a moment the possibility that the missing element can be introduced merely by adding "more form" and instead try to make a closer study of the facts, we soon come to the insight that the rationality of the object most often applies to a few of its characteristics but not to all. Originally rationalism meant something connected with the method of production. It is not certain that the first impetus for rational architecture was the production technique but it certainly was one of the first. If we think of a tubular metal chair, let us say one of Marcel Breuer's first models, we can clearly conclude: the impetus for its creation has its source in a series of interrelated desires to make pieces that would be lighter than before but just as comfortable and that, especially in their method of manufacture, are oriented to present-day methods of production. The finished product has above all received the imprint of the production method. To achieve a springy seat merely with a few bent tubes and some tightly stretched bits of leather is in itself a clever technical solution. It can in this regard justly be labeled rational. It can also be considered so in many other respects, primarily from a structural viewpoint. But a chair has an endless series of requirements that it should, when finished, fulfill and not till it fulfills all of them in a reasonable way, without different requirements coming into conflict with each other, can it be regarded a thoroughly rational creation. One can of course understand the word rational in a variety of ways, but the main criterion is fulfilling all the definable rational requirements so that they form a totality without conflict. If we wish to list the requirements that these chairs do not succeed in filling we could mention the following: a piece of furniture that forms a part of a person's daily habitat should not cause excessive glare from light reflection; ditto, it should not be disadvantageous in terms of sound, sound absorption, etc. A piece that comes into the most intimate contact with man, as a chair does, shouldn't be constructed of materials that are excessively good conductors of heat. I merely name these three criteria that the tubular metal chairs hardly fulfill. One could list a large number of additional requirements that in this particular case are not met. The main criticism against the metal chairs has been that they are not what one would call "cozy." This has in most cases been true, but when one uses the concept of coziness to mean something totally, undefinably human and claims that only traditional formalism could create it then one is on the wrong path. The criticisms, too noisy, too light-reflective, and too good a heat conductor, are in reality scientific terms for things that when put together form the mystical concept of "cozy."

It is apparent that among even the best rational creations of the new architecture there has been a lack of filling precisely such requirements as those listed above, which are the dearest to people and often are components of the requirements for which we have used emotionally tinged words.

In other words, we can say that one of the ways to arrive at a more and more humanely built environment is to expand the concept rational. We should rationally analyze more of the requirements connected with the object than we have to date. All the different requirements imaginable that can be made of an object's quality form a sort of scale, perhaps a series similar to a spectrum. In the red field of the spectrum lie social viewpoints, in the orange field questions connected with production, etc., all the way to the invisible ultraviolet field, where perhaps the rationally undefinable requirements, still invisible to us, which exist in the individual human being, are hidden. Whatever the case, it is at the end of the spectrum, where the purely human questions reside, where we will make most new discoveries. That these won't be limited to the random examples I mentioned for the metal chair is clear. Even if, as suggested above, we can find on closer analysis that an emotional concept is among other things a sum of physically measurable quantities, we still will quickly find ourselves outside the realm of physics. A series of requirements that can be made of almost every object and that up to now has been given scant consideration surely belongs in the sphere of another science—psychology. As soon as we include psychological requirements, or, let us say, when we can do so, then we will have already expanded the rational method to an extent that, to a greater degree than previously, has the potential of excluding inhuman results.

. . .

Each solution is in some way a compromise that is most easily discovered when one considers man in his weakest condition.

. . .

Instead we should expand the rational approach so that it includes more requirements connected to the problem. We should rationally examine the technical and the general hygienic needs all the way to that borderline where the psychological needs begin and even over this line to the best of

our abilities. That the experience of the long and rich tradition of the applied arts can here give us valuable study material is of course clear. I mean the genuine tradition and its historical development, but not the traditionalism that survives formally and inorganically.
. . .

I have tried to show that the rational work done during the manufacture and design of the objects has by no means led to its definite goal; that mistakes and weaknesses—they must be legion—are not of the type that dilettantism and grafting on of inorganic and questionable formal elements can help overcome. I have meant to say that the correct meaning of rationalism is to process all the questions that concern the object, to deal rationally also with the requirements that are often regarded as undefinable individual questions of taste but that on closer analysis show themselves to be partly neurological, partly psychological questions, etc. Salvation can come only or primarily through an expanded rationality.
. . .

As long as standardization is the production principle it should be regarded as highly inhumane to produce formalism. A standard article should not be a definitive product; it should on the contrary be made so that the form is completed by man himself according to all the individual laws that involve him. Only in the case of objects that have a neutral quality can standardization's coercion of the individual be softened and its positive side culturally exploited.
. . .

But even the psychological element in the new applied arts, within its rational working domain, if I may express it so, still exists in the Bronze Age. It is the purely social education of large masses of people that is lacking here; therefore formalism sold by advertising techniques still has a good market. People get objects with standardized forms and ready-made standardized decorations, which, because of these same characteristics, hinder them from creating an environment for themselves with a living, natural, constantly changing character.

We have thus come back to the question of "form as such." A constantly changing environment means that there is after all a form that should be independent of how things are constructed. We have already touched upon the importance of variability. Nature, biology, is formally rich and luxuriant. It can with the same structure, the same intermeshing, and the same principles in its cells' inner structure, achieve a billion combinations, each of which represents a high level of form. Man's life belongs to the same family. The things surrounding him are hardly fetishes and allegories with a mystical eternal value. They are rather cells and tissues, living beings also, building elements of which human life is put together. They cannot be treated differently from biology's other elements or otherwise they run the risk of not fitting into the system; they become inhuman.

"Rationalismen och människan" (Rationalism and Man)
Lecture given at the annual meeting of the Swedish Society of Crafts and Design, May 9, 1935

•

Every formal straitjacket, whether it be a deep-rooted stylistic tradition or a superficial uniformity born out of a misunderstanding of modern architecture, prevents architecture from playing its full part in the human struggle for existence; in other words, lessens its significance and effectiveness.

"Rakenteitten ja aineitten vaikutus nykyaikaiseen rakennustaiteeseen" (The Influence of Construction and Materials on Modern Architecture)
Lecture given at the Nordic Building Conference, Oslo, 1938

One of the typical activities in modern architecture has been the construction of chairs and the adoption of new materials and new methods for them. The tubular steel chair is surely rational from technical and constructive points of view: It is light, suitable for mass production, and so on. But steel and chromium surfaces are not satisfactory from the human point of view. Steel is too good a conductor of heat. The chromium surface gives too bright reflections of light, and even acoustically is not suitable for a room. The rational methods of creating this furniture style have been on the right track, but the result will be good only if rationalization is exercised in the selection of materials which are most suitable for human use.

The present phase of modern architecture is doubtless a new one, with the special aim of solving problems in the humanitarian and psychological fields.

This new period, however, is not in contradiction to the first period of technical rationalization. Rather, it is to be understood as an enlargement of rational methods to encompass related fields.

During the past decades architecture has often been compared with science, and there have been efforts to make its methods more scientific, even efforts to make it a pure science. But architecture is not a science. It is still the same great synthetic process of combining thousands of definite human functions, and remains architecture.

Its purpose is still to bring the material world into harmony with human life.

To make architecture more human means better architecture, and it means a functionalism much larger than the merely technical one. This goal can be accomplished only by architectural methods—by the creation and combination of different technical things in such a way that they will provide for the human being the most harmonious life.

Architectural methods sometimes resemble scientific ones, and a process of research, such as science employs, can be adopted also in architecture. Architectural research can be more and more methodical, but the substance of it can never be solely analytical. Always there will be more of instinct and art in architectural research.

. . .

Technical functionalism is correct only if enlarged to cover even the psychophysical field. That is the only way to humanize architecture.

Flexible wooden furniture is a result of experiments also made at the Paimio Sanatorium. At the time of those experiments the first tubular chromium furniture was just being constructed in Europe. Tubular and chromium surfaces are good solutions technically, but psychophysically these materials are not good for the human being. The sanatorium needed furniture that should be light, flexible, easy to clean, and so on. After extensive experimentation in wood, the flexible system was discovered and a method and material combined to produce furniture that was better for the human touch and more suitable as the general material for the long and painful life in a sanatorium.

The main problem connected with a library is that of the human eye. A library can be well constructed and can be functional in a technical way even without the solving of this problem, but it is not humanly and architecturally complete unless it deals satisfactorily with the main human function in the building, that of reading a book. The eye is only a tiny part of the human body, but it is the most sensitive and perhaps the most important part. To provide a natural or an artificial light that destroys the human eye or that is unsuitable for its use, means reactionary architecture even if the building should otherwise be of high constructive value.

"The Humanizing of Architecture," *Technology Review*, 1940

In this architecture there is, in addition to the decoration and ornament, another art form, more organic in its origin. It is mainly based on construction, jointing methods, and, for example, furniture joints. In this sense it is a distinctive art close to nature.

The art form of Karelian furniture is based, like the buildings proper, on the growing tree. While the tree's standard part, the trunk, is used for the buildings, the smaller but formally richer parts of the material, the naturally shaped branches and often even peculiar formations, are used for the furniture.

One would have to search to find an affinity to nature more logical in its beauty—the tall fir tree represents the building, its knotty branches and sculptural parts the furniture and movable parts.

And in this respect the Karelian building culture has an intimate contact with the present. I know from personal experience the time about ten years ago when "the fight against metal" in interior design was begun, though this business, as far as it concerned me, did not have its source in any sentimental Karelianism.

The Karelian furniture maker's art, which, because of the lack of technical aids, used parts ready-made by nature, achieved at its best a truly brilliant richness of forms and a surprising virtuosity in putting together nature's own shapes into an elegant and practical totality.

"Karjalan rakennustaide" (Architecture in Karelia), *Uusi Suomi*, 1941

•

Standardization involves industrial violence against individual taste.

"Kulttuuri ja tekniikka" (Culture and Technology), *Suomi-Finland—USA*, 1947

•

There are only two things in art—humanity or its lack. The mere form, some detail in itself, does not create humanity. We have today enough of superficial and rather bad architecture which is modern.
. . .

It does not matter how much electric cables or the wheels of motorcars are standardized, but when we come to the home, to the things that are close to us, the problem is different—it becomes a question of the spirit, it becomes a question of what intellectual standardization involves.

"The Architectural Struggle"
Transcript of a speech given to the Royal Institute of British Architects, 1957

119

201 *Sketch for the fan-shaped leg, 1954.*

120

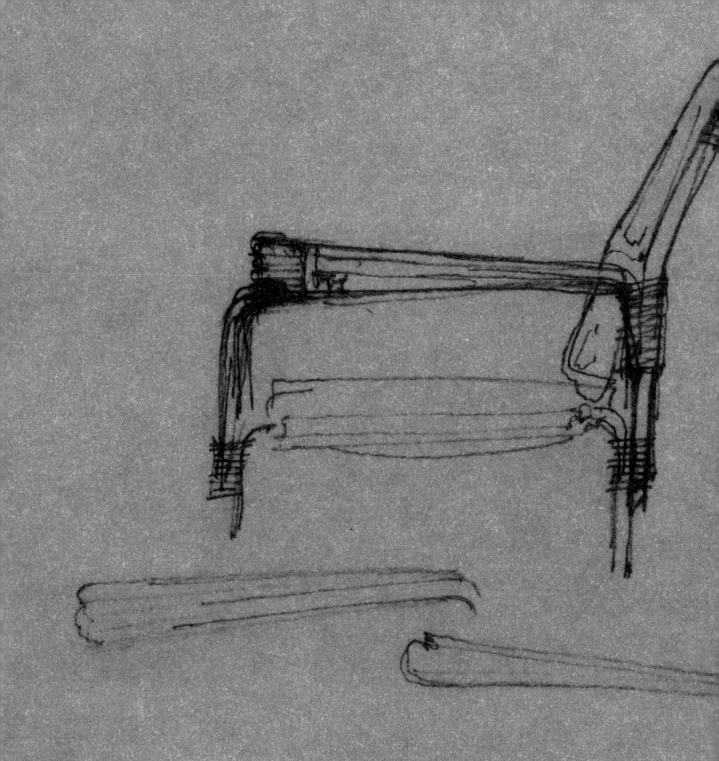

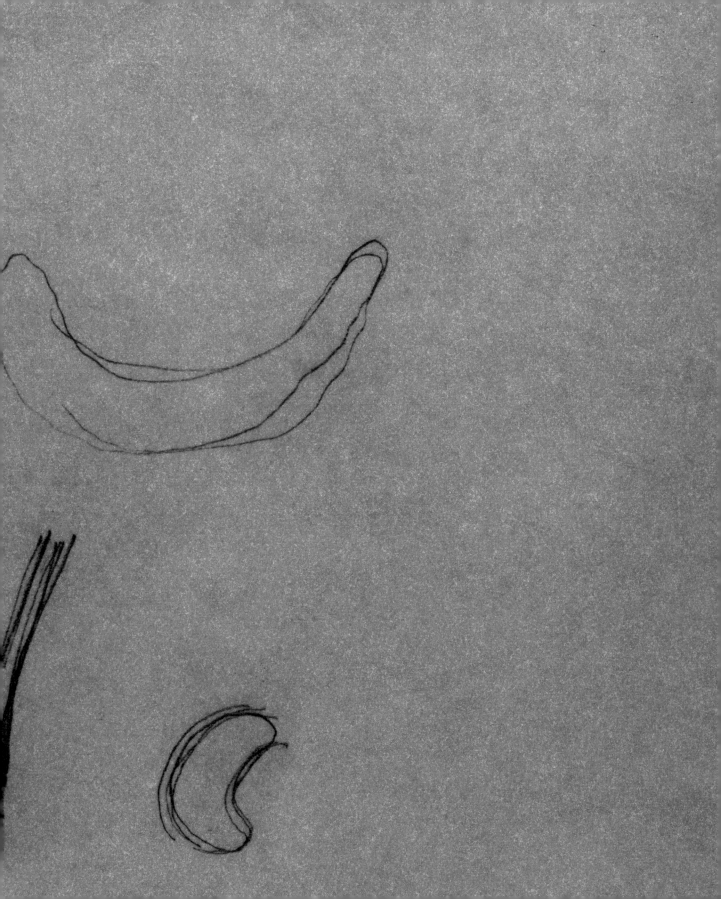

This list includes the most important models Aalto designed, mainly for industrial production, and generally made by Huonekalutehdas Korhonen Oy (formerly Huonekalu- ja Rakennustyötehdas Oy).

As very few original drawings have survived — and these usually undated — it has been necessary to estimate the date from such information as the project the furniture was planned for or pictures from exhibitions and interiors where the pieces appeared for the first time with certainty. It has not, therefore, been considered possible to draw up an exacting dating. Moreover, the long period between the planning and production processes supports this conclusion.

CHRONOLOGY OF STANDARD FURNITURE

1929 –1930

LINKED CHAIR 611

Birch, seat and back in plywood. Lacquered or painted. Later both seat and back upholstered or cross-woven in webbing. Stackable.

1929 Jyväskylä Civil Guards' House
1929 Turku 7th Centenary Exhibition

ARMCHAIR 15

Birch, laminated bent back curve, seat and back in plywood or upholstered. Stackable.

1929 Turku 7th Centenary Exhibition
1930 Minimum Apartment Exhibition, Helsinki

TABLE 96

Birch, straight legs.

1929 Turku 7th Centenary Exhibition
1930 Minimum Apartment Exhibition, Helsinki

ARMCHAIR

Moulded plywood back and seat from mahogany. Wooden legs painted black. Detachable mattress-like cover.

1929 Turku 7th Centenary Exhibition
1930 Minimum Apartment Exhibition, Helsinki; with tubular metal legs

CHAIR 23

Moulded plywood back and seat, tubular metal legs. Stackable.

1929 Turku 7th Centenary Exhibition

CHEST OF DRAWERS 296, 297

Birch, lacquered or painted. On plinth or wheels.

1930 Minimum Apartment Exhibition, Helsinki

202 *Sketch of the "macaroni" bent armchair for the National Pensions Institute head office, early 1950's.*

CONVERTIBLE SOFA

Metal frame, chromed or painted. Produced by Wohnbedarf AG, Zürich.

1930 Minimum Apartment Exhibition, Helsinki

TABLE

Six round nickel-plated metal shelves, metal base.

Aalto's flat, Turku

CHILDREN'S CHAIR

Moulded plywood, tubular metal legs. Aalto's flat, Turku

1931 –1932 ARMCHAIR

Seat, back and armrests from same moulded plywood. Tubular metal legs. Stackable.

Paimio Sanatorium

STOOL

Seat from plywood, metal legs. Stackable.

Paimio Sanatorium

ARMCHAIR 41

Laminated sides bent into closed curve. Seat and back from moulded plywood.

Paimio Sanatorium

ARMCHAIR 44

Same as 41 but sprung and upholstered.

Paimio Sanatorium

ARMCHAIR 403

Seat and back from moulded plywood. Birch legs. Stackable.

Paimio Sanatorium

TABLE 915

Laminated sides bent into a closed curve. Top from moulded plywood.

Paimio Sanatorium.

ARMCHAIR 31

Laminated cantilever frame. Seat and back from moulded plywood.

Paimio Sanatorium
1932 Nordic Building Exhibition, Helsinki

CHILDREN'S CHAIR 103

Moulded plywood, laminated bent leg.

1932 –1933 CHAIR 21

Plywood back and seat as in chair 23. Laminated bent leg.

BENT LEG (AALTO LEG)

Solid wood leg, bent at 90°, with bent part laminated. Fixed with screws. Used in different sizes in countless chair and table models, cupboards, beds, etc.

1933 Patented

STOOL 60

Round seat, three Aalto legs. Stackable.

1933 Fortnum and Mason's Exhibition, London

TABLE 70

Round table, hanging shelf. Four Aalto legs. Stackable.

1933 Fortnum and Mason's Exhibition, London

ARMCHAIR 402

Laminated cantilever supports as in armchair 31. Seat and back padded and upholstered.

1933 Milan Triennial

ARMCHAIR 401

High-backed version of armchair 402.

1933 Milan Triennial

**1933
–1935**

CHAIR 65

Round seat, four Aalto legs. Moulded plywood back.

Viipuri library

CHAIR K65

High chair, Round seat, four Aalto legs. Low moulded plywood back.

CHAIR 66

Same as chair 65, seat bigger, back higher.

CHAIR 68

Round seat, four Aalto legs, laminated bent back. Stackable.

Viipuri library

CHAIR 69

Otherwise same as chair 68, but seat not round. Wider back part.

CHAIR 62

As chair 69, seat and back padded and upholstered.

STOOL 64

High stool, round seat, four Aalto legs, laminated footrest ring.

**1935
–1936**

ARMCHAIR 400

Wide laminated cantilever supports. Seat and back sprung and upholstered. Also high-backed.

1936 Milan Triennial

SCREEN 100

Pine, rollable.

SHELF 111

Laminated bent sides, fixed into shelves.

SHELF 112

Triangular laminated consoles. Plywood shelf.

Consoles have also been used for clothes racks, umbrella stands, shelves with drawers, etc.

ARMCHAIR

High-backed upholstered armchair. Solid wood armrest and leg supports of the bent type.

1936 Arts and Crafts Exhibition, Helsinki

TEA TROLLEY 98

Laminated sides bent into a closed curve. Shelves veneered or covered with linoleum.

1936 Milan Triennial

**1936
–1937**

TEA TROLLEY 900

Laminated sides bent into closed curve as in tea trolley 98. Shelf tops tiled, wicker or rattan basket.

1937 Paris World Fair

ARMCHAIR 39

Laminated cantilever supports. Seat and back padded and upholstered. Later also cross-woven leather or webbing.

1937 Paris World Fair

**1938
–1939**

GARDEN TABLE 330, 332

White painted wood.

Villa Mairea

GARDEN CHAIR 310

White painted wood.

Villa Mairea

ARMCHAIR 406

Laminated cantilever supports as in armchair 31. Cross-woven webbing on seat and back.

Villa Mairea
1946—1947 present version in production

1946 –1947

Y LEG

A leg with two 90° bends, originally made from an Aalto leg sawn in two, but nowadays from a laminated bend.

Used in different sizes in chairs and tables.

STOOL Y61

Y-legged stool with cross-woven webbing or rattan seat, also quilted.

GLASS TABLE Y805

Y-legged table with removable glass top.

CHAIR 612

Y front legs continue into back upright. Solid wood back legs. Seat padded and upholstered, back quilted or cross-woven in webbing.

STOOL V63

Seat formed from laminated ring forming the frustum of a cone, rattan or quilted covering. The three legs formed from two ordinary Aalto legs bent at a sharper angle and screwed into the seat ring.

ARMCHAIR 45

Laminated armrest-leg supports. Seat and back parts bent into a closed curve, cross-woven in webbing or rattan, or quilted.

ARMCHAIR 46

Same leg construction as in armchair 45. Padded and upholstered seat and back.

ARMCHAIR 47

Similar leg construction as in armchair 45. Sprung and upholstered seat and back.

ARMCHAIR 48

Same as armchair 47.

CHAIR 67

Shape and construction as in chair 69 but laminated bent back support.

CHAIR

Y-legged chair, padded seat. Back formed from vertical laminated bent slats and horizontal webbing.

1947 Aalto Exhibition at Helsingin Taidehalli

1954

X LEG

Fan-shaped leg made from sawing an Aalto leg into five parts. Legs dowelled into seat or table-top.

1954 Aalto Exhibition, NK, Stockholm.

STOOL X600

Round seat, ash veneer or upholstered, 3 X legs.

STOOL X601

Square seat, ash veneer or upholstered,
4 X legs.

STOOL X602

Hexagonal seat, ash veneer or
upholstered, 3 X legs.

TABLE X800

X-legged table, ash or oak veneer.

GLASS TABLE

X-legged frame, removable glass top.

1955 ARMCHAIR

Solid wood structure assembled with
metal sockets. Removable cushions on
seat and back.

1955 H55 Exhibition, Helsingborg

1956 BRACKET LEG

Wooden table legs, fixed to top with
metal sockets. Three models.

National Pensions Institute head office,
Helsinki

ARMCHAIR

X legs, padded and upholstered seat
and back. Armrests made from
"macaroni" bends — thin sticks of
birch, bent in bunches.

National Pensions Institute head office,
Helsinki

1959 ARMCHAIR

Sprung and upholstered frame, armrest-
leg structure from "macaroni" bends.

La Maison Louis Carré, France

CHAIR 611

Stackable linked chair, first used in the Jyväskylä Civil Guards' House in 1929. Birch, seat and back originally plywood, nowadays padded and upholstered, or cross-woven in webbing.

203

130

cm | 10 | 20 | 30 | 40 | 50 |

ARMCHAIR 41

Designed for the Paimio Sanatorium, 1931—1932. Laminated birch sides bent into a closed curve. Seat and back from moulded plywood painted black or white, originally also with curly-grained or ordinary birch veneer and lacquered. (206)

ARMCHAIR 44

Sprung and upholstered version of armchair 41, also for the Paimio Sanatorium. (205)

132

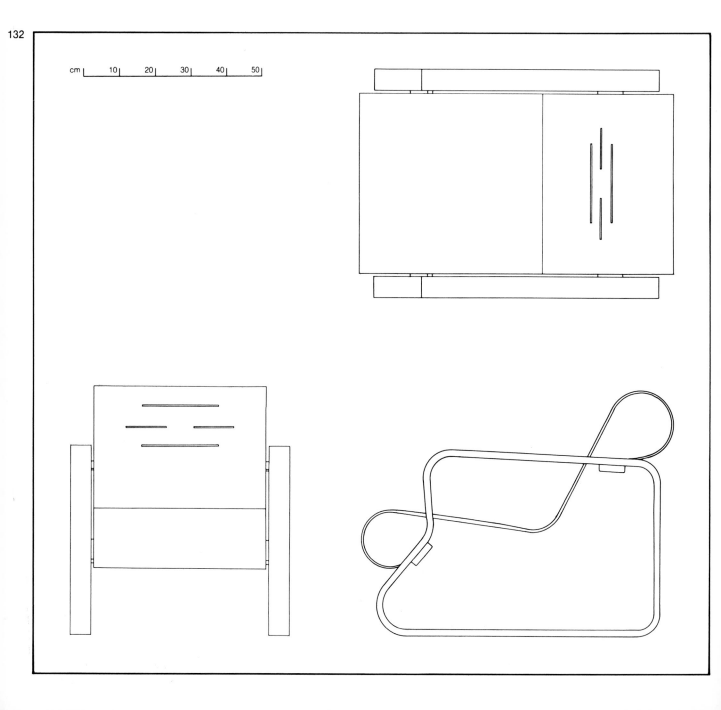

cm | 10 | 20 | 30 | 40 | 50 |

ARMCHAIR 403

Stackable armchair designed for the
Paimio Sanatorium, 1931—1932.
Birch legs, seat and back from moulded
plywood, natural colour or painted
white or black. Later also padded and
upholstered.

207

cm | 10 | 20 | 30 | 40 | 50 |

TABLE 915

Designed for the Paimio Sanatorium,
1931—1932.
Laminated birch sides bent into a
closed curve. Top from moulded
plywood, natural colour or painted
white or black.

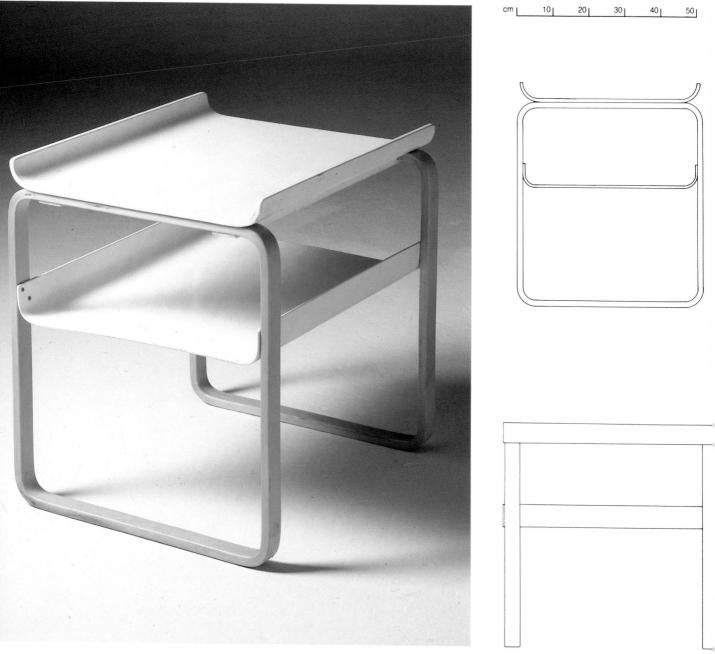

ARMCHAIR 31

Designed for the Paimio Sanatorium
1931—32. Shown at the Nordic
Building Exhibition in Helsinki, 1932.
Laminated birch cantilever sides.
Seat and back from moulded plywood,
painted black or white. Also with curly-
grained or ordinary birch veneer and
lacquered. (213)

ARMCHAIR 402

Armchair exhibited at the Milan Triennial, 1933. Same cantilever sides as in
armchair 31. Seat and back padded
and upholstered. (211)

ARMCHAIR 401

High-backed version of armchair 402,
also exhibited at the Milan Triennial,
1933. (212)

138

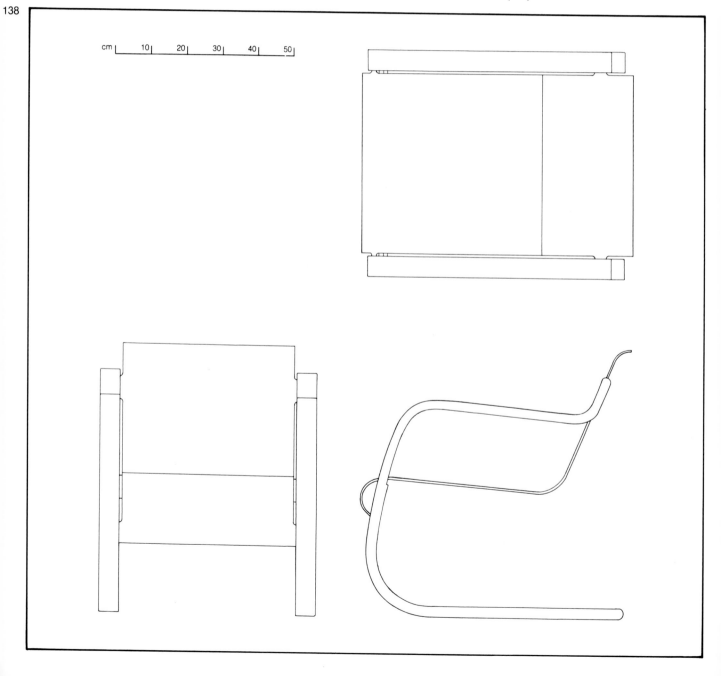

cm 10 20 30 40 50

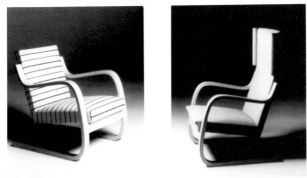

211

212

213

STOOL 60

Stackable stool from 1932—33, displayed at the London Exhibition in 1933. Round seat covered with plywood, linoleum or plastic laminate. Also padded and upholstered. Three bent Aalto legs.

142

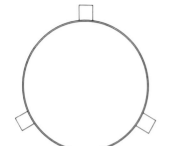

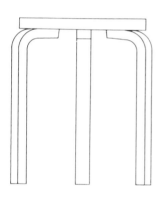

STOOL 64

High, four-legged stool; structure as in stool 60. Footrest ring from laminated bent birch.

215

216

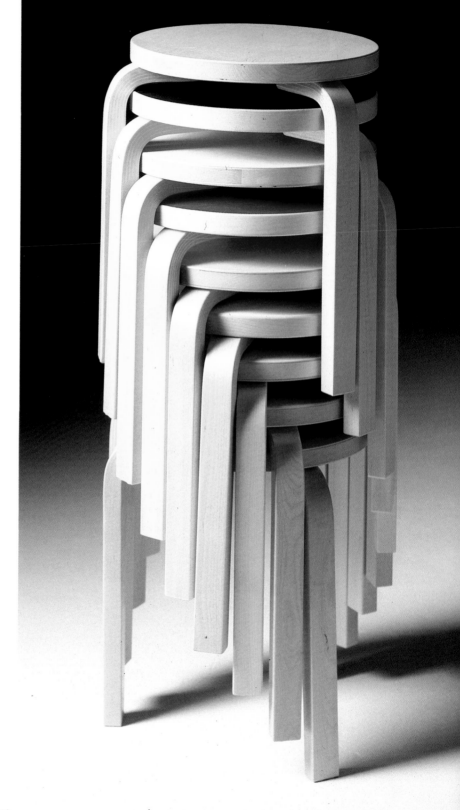

CHAIR 65

Chair used, for example, in Viipuri library, 1933—35. Same structure as in stool 60.
Moulded plywood back screwed to back legs.

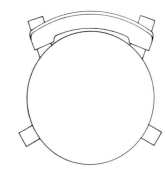

143

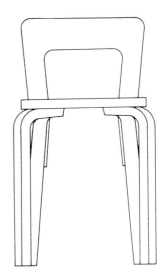

144 HIGH CHAIR K65

Same structure as chair 65. (218)

CHAIR 66

Same structure as chair 65. Often also painted black. (219)

CHAIR 68

Same structure as chair 65 but back from laminated bent birch. Stackable. (220)

CHAIR 69

Basically same structure as above but only plywood or upholstered seat. (221)

218

219

220

221

TEA TROLLEY 900

Tea trolley from 1936—37. Laminated
birch side supports, bent into a closed
curve.
Top surfaced with white or black tiles.
Rattan or wicker basket. (223)

TEA TROLLEY 98

Same structure as tea trolley 900 but
shelves from birch veneer or covered
with linoleum or plastic laminate.
(222)

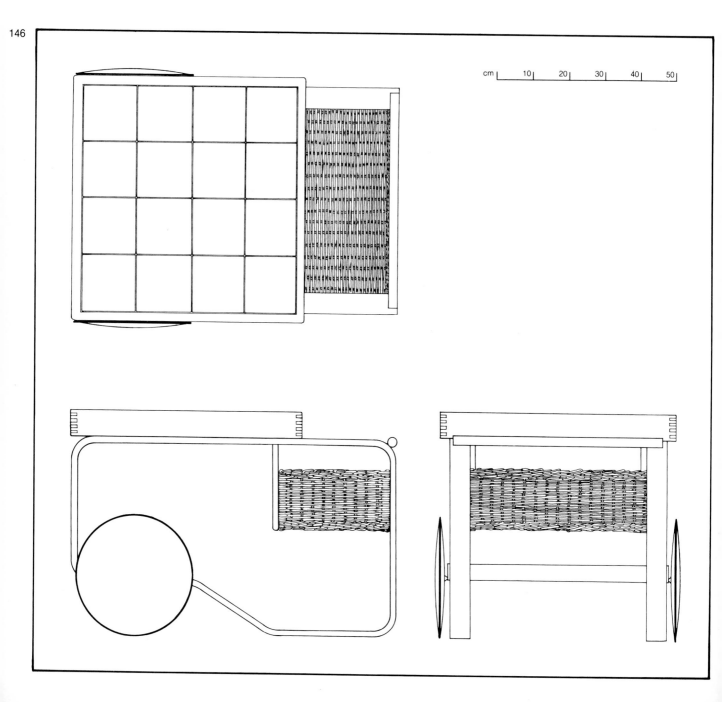

cm 10 20 30 40 50

222

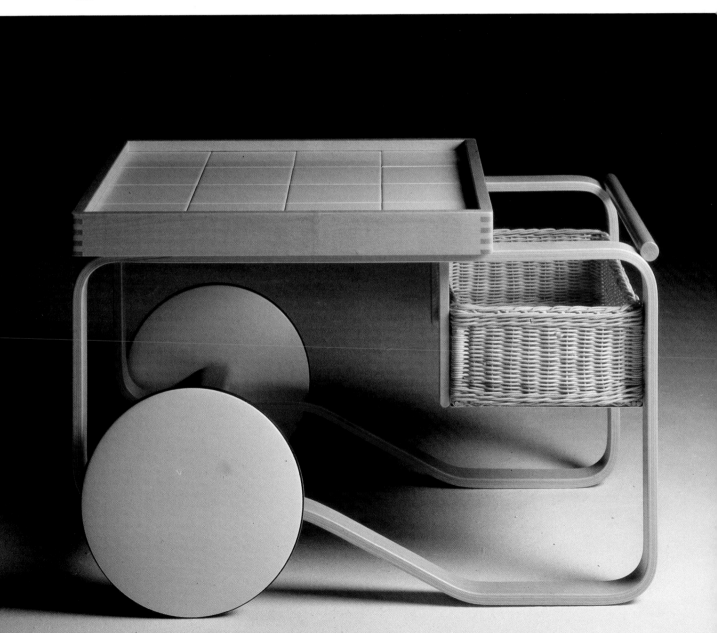

223

ARMCHAIR 400

Armchair from 1935—36.
Laminated birch cantilever sides.
Seat and back sprung and
upholstered.

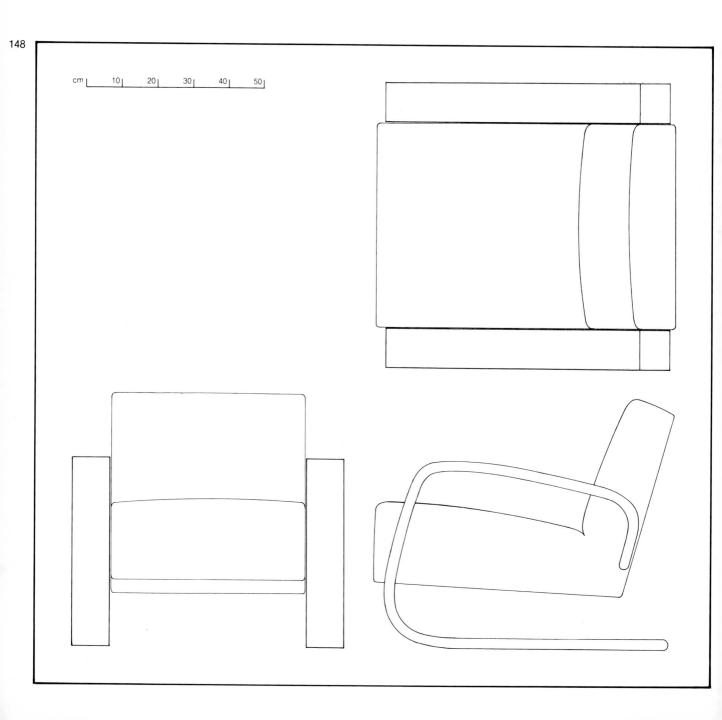

224

225

ARMCHAIR 39

Armchair from 1936—1937, first shown
in the Finnish Pavilion designed by
Aalto for the Paris World Fair.
Laminated birch cantilever sides.
Same technique used for seat and
back frame, cross-woven in webbing
or leather, originally padded and
upholstered.

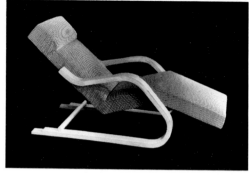

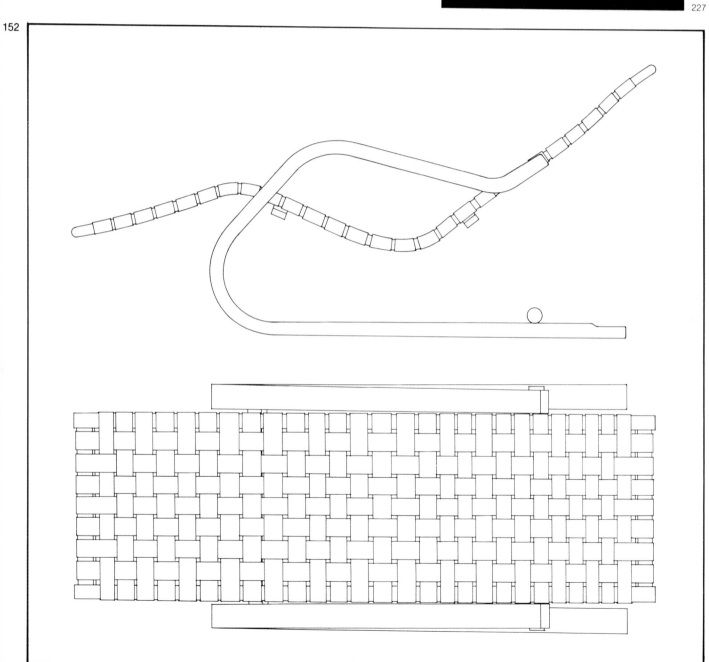

ARMCHAIR 45

Armchair from 1946—1947.
Laminated armrest-leg structure. Seat
and back in frame construction,
cross-woven in webbing or rattan.
Alternatively in quilted leather or canvas. Armrests bound in rattan or
leather. (233)

154 ARMCHAIR E45

Variant of chair 45 from 1962.
Padded and upholstered seat and
back. (229)

ARMCHAIR 46

Same leg structure as 45 but seat and
back padded and upholstered
throughout. (230)

ARMCHAIR 47

Similar leg structure as 45.
Sprung and upholstered seat and
back. (231)

ARMCHAIR 48

Variant of armchair 47. (232)

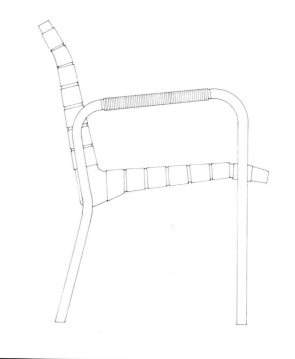

229

230

231

232

STOOL Y61

Stackable stool from 1946—1947.
Y leg, a leg bent at two 90° angles,
originally made from an Aalto leg
sawn in two but nowadays from a
laminated bend.
Seat cross-woven in webbing or rattan.
Alternatively upholstered in leather
quilting or canvas.

GLASS TABLE Y805

Same leg structure as in stool Y61.
Removable glass top.

234

156

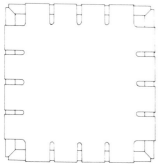

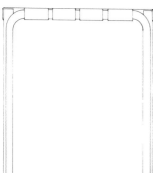

cm | 10| 20| 30| 40| 50|

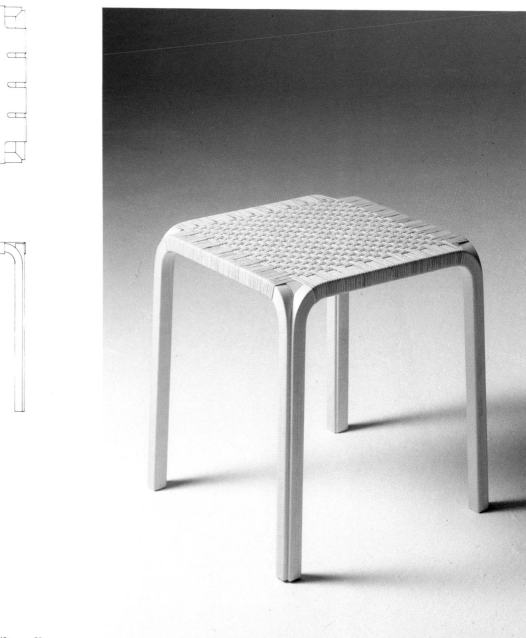

CHAIR 612

Stackable chair from 1946—1947.
Laminated Y leg structure as in stool
Y61. Legs continue to form back
uprights. Back legs from solid wood.
Seat padded and upholstered, back
cross-woven in webbing, or quilted.

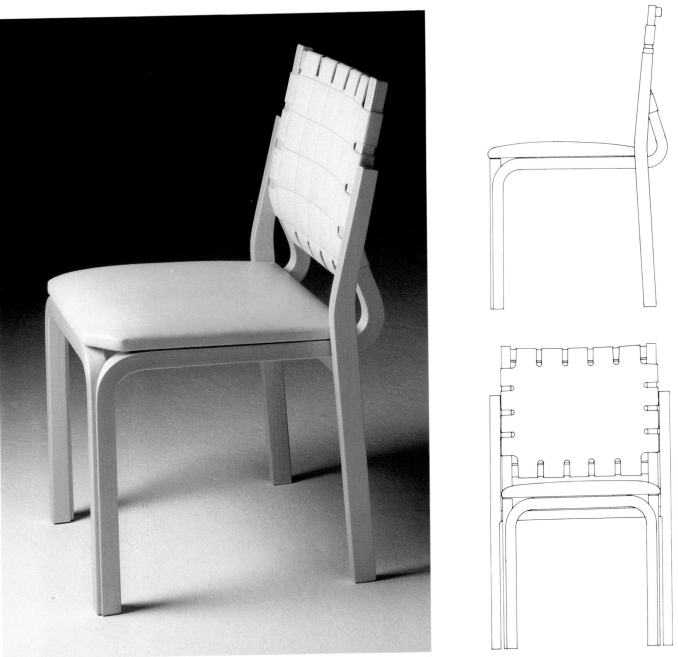

ARMCHAIR 406

Variant of armchair 31. First version
1938—39, final 1946—47.
Laminated seat and back frame,
cross-woven in webbing or rattan.
Alternatively in quilted leather or
canvas.

158

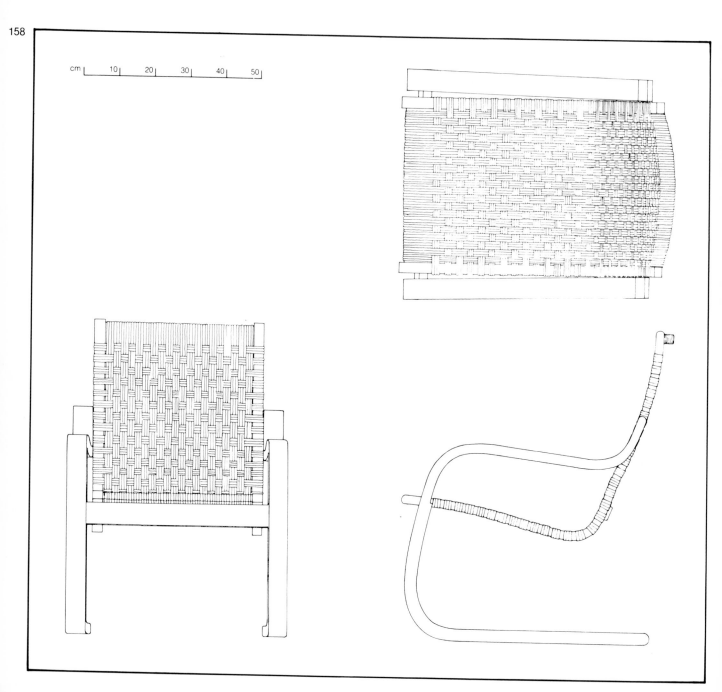

STOOL X601

Stool from 1954.
Fan-shaped X leg, made by sawing
Aalto leg into five pieces. Legs dowelled
into seat, which is covered with ash
veneer or upholstered in leather.

160   cm | 10 | 20 | 30 | 40 | 50 |

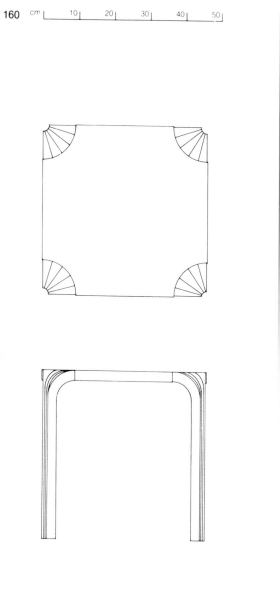

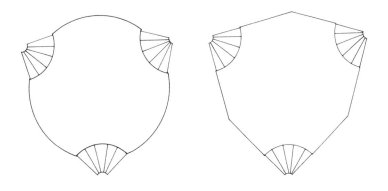

STOOL X600

Round stool, structure as in X601.

STOOL X602

Hexagonal stool, structure as in X601.

239

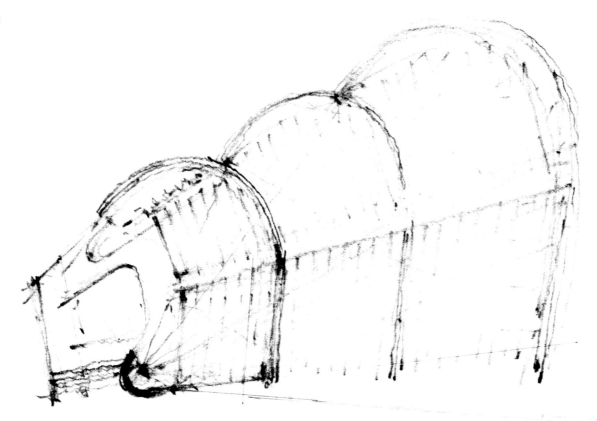

240 *Sketches for the Vuoksenniska church, executed in 1958.*

FIXED FURNITURE IN ALVAR AALTO'S ARCHITECTURE

Elissa Aalto & Marja-Riitta Norri

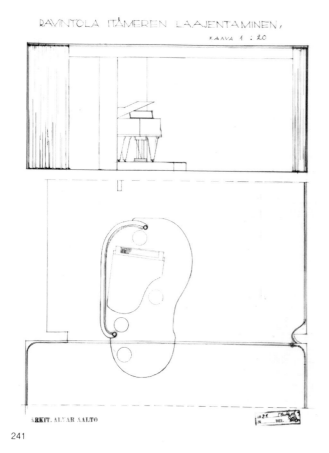

RAVINTOLA ITÄMEREN LAAJENTAMINEN,
KAAVA 1 : 20

ARKIT. ALVAR AALTO

241

A striving towards an overall concept in planning buildings is already recognizable in Alvar Aalto's early works; interiors were an essential part of the architectural wholeness. A considerable number of the drawings for almost all buildings concerned fixed interiors. These elements, though not actual furniture, often give the basic expression to the space.

Functional considerations are primary in Alvar Aalto's fixed interior design work; form is never an end in itself. The appreciation of objects and furnishings is the principal influence in the selection of materials, although durability is also a major factor. The limits imposed by technology are also present, subconsciously, via experience and experimentation.

In studying different structural alternatives, each case was discussed with the manufacturer to find the simplest solution. Prototype testing was carried out on objects for which no experience was known.

Each project is a unique entity with its own special demands and delineations. Even so, as there are certain features common to interiors serving the same purpose, it is possible to trace the lines of development taking shape in his solutions to the problems of space and detail.

We have chosen here some examples of interior solutions for civic buildings planned for different purposes as well as one of a private house.

Fixed furnishings designed for a specific building were often supplemented by Aalto's mass-produced furniture. These, too, had frequently been originally designed for a certain project.

The planning stage of many of Alvar Aalto's buildings lasted several years. In this article the design year given for each interior work is that for when the building was completed because the detailed planning of the furnishings usually took place whilst construction was going on.

241 *Free-form orchestra stand of the Itämeri restaurant in the Agricultural Co-operative building, Turku 1928. The idea behind the shape was that dancing couples would not bump themselves on the corners.*

242- *Paimio Sanatorium (1933)*
245 *Alvar Aalto designed both the fixed furnishings and movable furniture for the Paimio Sanatorium — the latter actually began in connection with this project. Technical equipment and fixtures were also developed to meet the specific requirements of the patients and the hygienic demands of the sanatorium. Examples of these are the noiseless wash basins, the ceiling radiators in the patients' rooms, the rounded edges of the wardrobes, beds, night tables and fittings, and the bent plywood chairs.*

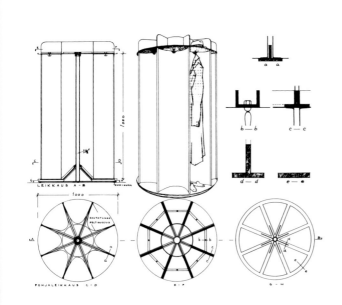

242

244

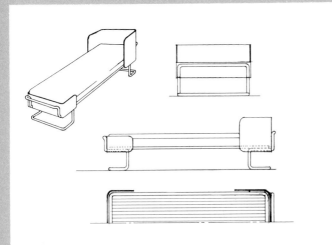

ARKIT. ALVAR AALTO   243

245

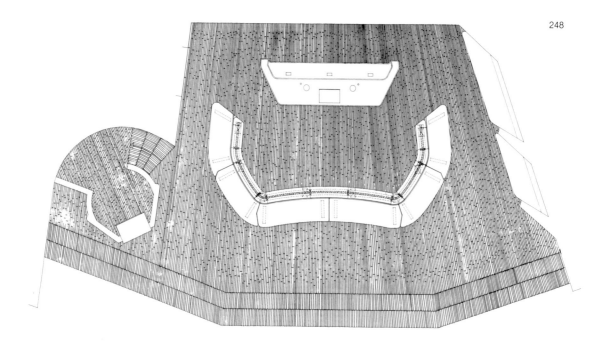

CHURCH INTERIORS

It is particularly important with churches that the furnishings should conform with the space and emphasize its architectonic form. There are considerable variations in Alvar Aalto's church interior solutions. The earliest of these was the Muurame church (1929). It has a fascinating and beautiful detail: candelabra at the aisle ends of the pews. The light fittings were designed by Poul Henningsen. Later on Aalto also designed the lights.

In the interiors for the Vuoksenniska (1958) and Seinäjoki (1960) churches there are similarities in the selection of materials: for example, the flooring in both was terra cotta tiling and marble was used for the chancels. The insides of the churches, however, are quite different in character. The space dictates the scale of the interior architecture: the chancel area is part of the whole and must, therefore, conform with the overall environment. The inside of the Seinäjoki church is huge and cathedral-like, whereas that of Vuoksenniska is more intimate.

The chancel areas of the churches with their pulpits, altar rails and kneeling benches, the lights, pews and organ facades were all designed in Aalto's office. The tapestries for the Vuoksenniska church were woven by Greta Skogster-Lehtinen from designs made in the office; Seinäjoki's tapestries were created in collaboration with a local textile designer. The organs in both churches were positioned in galleries; at the rear of the nave in Seinäjoki and beside the chancel in Vuoksenniska.

Vuoksenniska was originally planned to serve various purposes. As the different areas also had to function as one they were separated by sliding partitions that curved into the walls.

The difference in design considerations between the Roman Catholic church at Riola and a Lutheran church is seen most clearly in the layout of the chancel area. The services are different: the importance of the sermon in a Lutheran church is replaced by the liturgy in a Roman Catholic one. Thus the Riola church has only a lectern for bible readings. Music also plays a vital role in the ceremonies; the organ and tiered choir stalls are positioned near the altar — a similar trend is noticeable in the newer Lutheran churches. Also the pews had to be equipped with a lower, kneeling bench.

248

246- *Vuoksenniska Church (1958)*
249   The flooring material in this church was terra cotta tile. As it was
       also desired that the floor of the raised chancel be white, narrow
       marble blocks of different lengths were used. Marble was also
       used for the altar rails and pulpit. The shape of the black leather
       upholstered kneeling bench was determined by practical con-
       siderations: to get as many places as possible in the rather small
       chancel area. The church tapestries were executed by Greta
       Skogster-Lehtinen from designs made in Aalto's office.

250 *Riola Church (1978)*
     In the Roman Catholic church at Riola the lectern has replaced the
     pulpit of the Lutheran church. The organ and tiered choir stalls are
     positioned close to the altar. The pews have a lower, kneeling
     bench.

251 *Muurame Church (1929)*
     The original interior designed by Aalto contained an interesting
     and beautiful detail: candelabra at the aisle ends of the pews.
     The lamps were designed by Poul Henningsen, though in later
     churches Aalto also designed the light fittings.

252 *Seinäjoki Church (1960)*
     The interior of the Seinäjoki church is like a cathedral. The space
     dictates the scale of the architecture. Red tiles have been used for
     the flooring; with some marble in the chancel, mainly on the pulpit.
     The church tapestries were created in collaboration with a Seinä-
     joki textile designer. The ceiling lights were specially designed for
     this church.

249

250

251

252

253, *Viipuri Town Library (1935)*
254 *Console shelving has been used in the lending room of the library instead of bookcases in order to avoid the need for upright supports. The baluster between the upper and lower floor levels also functions as a reading desk. The tables in the reading room have been joined by a bent plywood structure which provides the reader with a place for his case and papers. The development of chairs and tables, which began during the later stage of the Paimio project, reaches its final form in the Viipuri library.*

253

255 *National Pensions Institute Library, Helsinki (1956)*
The library of the National Pensions Institute is a small, specialized one in which the principles involved in the space solution of the Viipuri library have been applied.

256 *Seinäjoki Town Library (1965)*
The positioning of the bookcases emphasizes the shape of the room. Light enters through windows high up on the walls rather than through skylights, and the outsides have bars across them to prevent excessive sunlight.

LIBRARIES

The first of Alvar Aalto's series of libraries was in Viipuri (1935). The floor in the centre part of the lending and reading room area is dropped so as to give a commanding view from the supervising librarian's desk. Aalto used the same solution in several of his later libraries, further enrichening the form of the room as that the view opened like a fan from the desk.

Another important factor was the arrangement of the lighting. In nearly all libraries the main source of light came in different forms from the ceilings. The round skylights in the main room of the Viipuri library dispersed light evenly throughout the room leaving the walls free for books.

Fixed furnishings predominated in library interiors. The positioning of the bookcases emphasized the shape of the room. The librarian's desks, card index cabinets and other essential furnishings formed a conspicuous part of the interior. The main considerations in design were functional convenience and environmental compatibility, not structure. Though each bookcase was bespoken for its own library there were no radical breakthroughs in structures. Console bookracks were employed in Viipuri, but even so most shelves had vertical supports and ends, the advantage being that they could be easily adjusted. The tables and shelves were from wood but the former were often surfaced with linoleum.

The interior of the Mount Angel Benedictine abbey library in Oregon, USA (1970), combined individual design with standard models. To give an original touch, wooden slat ends were designed in Aalto's office for the standard American metal bookracks.

255

256

254

257 *Rovaniemi Town Library (1968)*
In most of Aalto's libraries the floors of the lending and reading rooms have been dropped a little to facilitate supervision and enrichen the shape of the spaces.

258 *Helsinki University of Technology Library (1969)*
The space solution here differs from Aalto's other libraries in that there is no variation in levels in the lending and reading rooms. The reading rooms are separated from the lending room, but the bookcases have been so positioned that overall supervision is retained.

259 *Wolfsburg Cultural Centre Library (1963)*

260 *Mount Angel Benedictine Abbey Library (1970)*
The library has been built on the side of a steep slope, a fact which has influenced its overall design: from the entrance side the building appears low and modest, but in the centre, where the full height has been utilized, the impression is one of great space. Also the light coming in through the complex roof structures add to the feeling of airiness. It functions in much the same way as town libraries and there are a number of study cubicles. The supervision desks were designed in Aalto's office, as, too, were the ribbed wooden ends to the standard American metal book-racks. Some of the light fittings were made in Finland and Aalto's furniture was used for the public areas, though American models for furnishing the other rooms.

257

259

258

260

261 *Helsinki University of Technology, Main Building, Entrance Hall (1964)*
262 *Öland limestone was used for the floor, marble for the cloakroom counters proved most durable, seen here with oak edging. Part of the pillars and walls have been faced with a special vitrified tile designed in Aalto's office. These are rod-like in form and almost semi-circular in profile.*

ENTRANCE HALLS

The first impression of a building is given by the entrance hall. This is conveyed mainly by materials and a sensation of space, as little can be said about furnishings consisting, as they usually do, of only the porter's desk or information counter, a group of chairs and a clothes-rack. The clothes-racks in the entrances to Aalto's buildings were designed and located to be as inconspicuous as possible.

The primary consideration in designing a cloakroom counter is its measurement: it is difficult to achieve an optimum length in a straight form. The public must also be considered: a curved shape is more agreeable than a rectangular and service is smoother.

The materials in entrance halls are exposed to hard wear: durability is thus of primary importance. For this reason vitrified bricks or tiles have been much used for protecting the surfaces of walls and pillars. Aalto's office designed special tile shapes for the Arabia porcelain factory in Helsinki. The first types were rectangular with rounded vertical edges. Later tiles had an almost semicircular profile with smaller sizes for interiors and larger for facades. The Arabia factory's art department was very skilled at producing different coloured glazings. Ceramic rods of varying colours were used for the interior of the National Pensions Institute building in Helsinki.

In addition to durability it is also important that the material should age beautifully. The main building of the Helsinki University of Technology has remained in good condition despite enduring almost twenty years of hard service. The choice of materials was simple and straightforward. The halls have the cheapest natural rock floors available: Öland limestone. A certain amount of ceramic tiling has, however, been used on the pillars. The ends of the clothes-racks are from slats of oak, the cloakroom counter top is from marble and the fronts are covered in linen.

In the entrance foyer of Finlandia Hall metal rings and not tiles have been used to protect the pillars: a more graceful solution for pillars that appear rather stout relative to the lowness of the space. The ends of the metal clothes-racks are metal-rimmed laminates. Clothes-racks from metal are preferred as they offer the desired strength with minimal measurements. The cloakroom counters in the foyer of Finlandia Hall are an adaptation of a structure widely used elsewhere: the legs consist of bunches of three metal tubes. Box-like elements have been built around the legs to form shelves on the inside for bags and boots, concealed from the public by linking front panels.

261

262

263 *Helsinki University of Technology, Library Foyer (1969)*
The same principles have been followed in selecting materials as in the entrance hall to the main building.

264 *Finlandia Hall, Lobby (1975)*
The pillars in the lobby of Finlandia Hall have been protected with metal rings. The ends of the metal clothes-racks are metal rimmed laminates. The cloakroom counters are box-like elements resting on bunches of tubular legs with panels joining them on the front side.

265 *Seinäjoki Town Hall, Entrance Hall (1965)*

266 *Rovaniemi Town Library, Entrance Hall (1968)*

267 *Wolfsburg Cultural Centre, Entrance Hall (1963)*
The clothes-racks in the entrance hall of the Wolfsburg Cultural Centre have ribbed wood ends. Profile has also been used on the fronts of the cloakroom counters.

263

265

264

266

268 *Helsinki University of Technology, Main Building, Main Auditorium (1964)*
The wall panelling is based on acoustic considerations. The desk flaps slide into the backs of the seats in front.

269 *Helsinki University of Technology, Public Lecture Hall (1964)*

174   AUDITORIUMS

Wooden panelling has frequently been used for covering the walls of lecture halls and meeting rooms. Their use in lecture rooms is based primarily on acoustic considerations: such surfaces partly absorb and partly reflect sound. Moreover, wood gives the room a warmer feeling and more dignified character than plain white walls. The design of meeting rooms in particular is based on an overall plan in which all the interior elements and materials are in harmony with each other.

Lecture halls and meeting rooms also require different kinds of tables or desks on the platforms. Each has its own special character: the ordinary platform speaker's lectern does not need any complex technical devices, whereas the podium desk in a lecture hall may well contain a great array of AV controls. The front dominates their overall appearance and this is often covered with profile strips.

The fixed seating in lecture halls usually has a flap-top desk attached, as in the auditoriums of the Helsinki University of Technology. The upholstery of the seats in the main auditorium is still the original, hardwearing fabric; the wooden parts, on the other hand, have had to be cleaned and restored.

269

268

270 *Helsinki University of Technology, Staff Meeting Room (1964)*
The interior is based on an overall plan in which all the individual elements are in harmony with each other. The profile panelling on the walls is for both acoustic and aesthetic reasons. Ribbed wood has been used on the front of the chairman's table.

271 *National Pensions Institute, Board of Administration Meeting Room (1956)*

272 *Säynätsalo Town Hall, Council Chamber (1952)*

273 *Alajärvi Town Hall, Council Chamber (1969)*

270

272

271

273

274, *Rautatalo Office Building, Café (1955)*
275 *The photo is of the original interior with its wooden panelled ceiling, later changed to a metal one to improve ventilation. The ceramic tiles, designed in Aalto's office, used here on the walls and counter, appear for the first time in the Rautatalo. A special feature of the café is the sound of water tumbling from one level to the next in the fountain.*

276 *National Pensions Institute, Open-Plan Office (1956)*
The main office of the National Pensions Institute is an open-plan designed space divided by low partitions into cubicles. The room was originally the Helsinki office where people came to discuss their pensions matters with officials in privacy. Now the purpose has been changed: the former service area open to the general public has now been cut off from the entrance hall by a glass wall and changed into an open-plan office. The partitions, beautifully carpentered with brass intarsia, have, fortunately, been allowed to remain despite the fact that the area is now too small to take today's display terminals and other office machines. Even with these, progress is towards smaller sizes and the trend is for more enclosed working areas within open-plan offices.

274

275

276

277- *Maison Louis Carré (1958)*
279 *A beautiful Ile de France view opens up from the lounge. Sliding wooden frames covered in cloth protect the room against excessive sunlight.*

The pine profile used on the lounge and hallway ceilings was brought from Säynätsalo. Some of the furniture was specially designed for this house.

The row of cupboards dividing the hallway serve as a background for pictures on the hall side and storage space on the bedroom side.

PRIVATE HOUSE

In designing a private house the architect must live the part of the client and become familiar with his way of life. The relationship is far more personal than when planning a public building. The Maison Louis Carré was planned down to the last detail — not merely because Alvar Aalto strived to create an harmonious whole but also because of Louis Carré's own wishes. Louis Carré probably took the same care in choosing his architect as the artists in his gallery, in order to prevent conflicts in stylistic outlook.

All the planning work was done in Aalto's office. Some of the furnishings were made in Finland, others in France. The narrow pine profile for the entrance hall and lounge ceilings was brought from Säynätsalo in Finland — as were the carpenters. The furniture, some of which was specially designed for this house, the light fittings and door handles were made in Finland. The library shelves, kitchen and annexes, closets and cupboards, on the other hand, were made in France.

The whole interior is characterized by the use of wood and this is further accentuated by their light and dark contrasting. This begins already with the inside doors, surfaced in ash with teak edging, and continues into the lounge with its mixture of ash and teak furniture.

278

279

277

178   IGOR HERLER'S ESSAY:

Alvar Aalto drawing archives   5c, 7, 8d, 9b, 11a, 12c, 13a, 14b, 15b, 15c, 16b, 18b, 19b, 20a, 21a, 21b (redrawn by I. H.), 22a, 22b, 23b, 24a (redrawn by I. H.), 24b, 25b, 26b, 26c, 26d, 27, 28b, 29, 33a, 34a, 34b (redrawn by I. H.), 36b, 36c, 37b, 37c, 38a, 38b, 40b, 41a, 42b, 43b, 44b, 45a, 46b (redrawn by I. H.), 47a, 47b, 48b.

Erkki Peräinen archives   8b, 8c, 10b, 11b, 17a.

Jyväskylä Town Parish Archives   8a, 49a, 49b.

Museum of Architecture, Stockholm   50a.

National Archives / National Board of Public Construction Drawing Archives   39b.

Igor Herler's measurement drawings and illustrations   2a, 6, 9c, 12b, 12d, 15a, 15d, 19a, 23a, 28c, 31a, 32, 36d, 37a, 39a, 43a, 44c, 48a, 51a, 53b.

Helsinki City Museum / Photo by E. Sundström   4a.

National Board of Antiquities and Historical Monuments / Photo by A. Pietinen   31b.

Photographic Museum of Finland / Photo by H. Cronström   33b.

Photo by Igor Herler   2b, 5b, 10a, 13b, 14c, 16c, 17b, 17c, 18c, 19c, 20b, 22c, 22e, 44a.

Photo by Jussi Tiainen   35.

G. M. Ellwood: *Möbel und Raumkunst in England 1680—1800*. Stuttgart 1913.   25a (redrawn by I. H.).

A. Koeppen — C. Breuer: *Geschichte des Möbels*. Berlin, New York 1904. 36a (mirror image).

L. V. Lockwood: *Amerikanische Möbel der Kolonialzeit*. Stuttgart 1917. 3a, 14a, 16a, 28a (perspective correction by I. H.), 40a, 42a, 46a, 52c, 54a, 54c (perspective correction by I. H.).

C. Malmsten: *Teckningar till enklare möbeltyper, häfte I*. Stockholm 1926.   4b.

W. Nutting: *Furniture Treasure*. New York 1954.   26a.

V. C. Salomonsky: *Masterpieces of Furniture*. New York 1953.   18a (redrawn by I. H.).

H. Schmitz: *Deutsche Möbel des Klassizismus*. Stuttgart 1923.   41b.

H. Schmitz: *Das Möbelwerk*. Berlin [1926].   22d.

G. Strengell: *Hemmet som konstverk*. Helsingfors 1923.   50b.

E. Wettergren: *L'art décoratif moderne en Suède*. Malmö 1925.   5d.

Aktiebolaget H. Bukowskis konsthandel, Stockholm. Auktionen den 24 och 25 september 1923. Stockholm 1923.   9a (mirror image).

David Blomberg, Stockholm [furniture catalogue]. 1922.   12a (redrawn by I. H.), 52a.

David Blomberg, Stockholm [furniture catalogue]. Malmö 1927.   3b.

Huonekaluja, neljäs sarja. (Tietosanakirja-osakeyhtiön käsiteollisuuspiirustuksia n:o 13). Helsinki 1924.   2c (redrawn by I. H.).

Kotiliesi 1925/5.   5a, 30 (both redrawn by I. H.).

Kotitaide 1915/3.   45b.

Käsiteollisuus 1925/2.   51b, 52b, 52d, 53a, 54b, 54d (all redrawn by I. H.).

Maaseudun Sanomat 22.6.1922.   1.

OTHER ESSAYS:

Alvar Aalto drawing archives   76—78, 92—97, 145—147, 201, 202, 240—243, 246—248, 250, page 11.

Alvar Aalto Museum, Jyväskylä   102, 106, 136 (all by Martti Kapanen).

Artek archives   75, 79, 80, 82, 84, 85, 86(Martti Malinen), 87b, 88, 90(Fred Runeberg), 100(H. Iffland), 101, 103(Kolmio), 104(Saurén), 109(Pietinen), 110—111(Max Petrelius), 112—115, 117, 118, 119(H. Iffland), 120(Pietinen), 121(Ilmari Kostiainen), 122(Saurén), 123(Pietinen), 124, 125, 126—129(Ilmari Kostiainen), 130, 131—132(H. Havas), 133(Pietinen), 134(Kolmio), 135(Wahlberg), 137(Kolmio), 139(Fox Photos, London), 140—141(Stab. fot. Crimella, Milano), 142—143(Studio Henry Sarian, Paris), 144(Museum of Modern Art, New York), 148, 149(Pietinen), 150(Stig Bergström), 151,

152(Max Petrelius), 154, 155(H. Havas), 156(Saurén), 157, 158(Pietinen), 159, 160(Mikko Karjanoja), 161, 162—163(Wahlberg), 164(Max Petrelius), 165—166(Kolmio), 167(Mannelin), 168, 169, 170—172(Mannelin), 173—179(Jukka Korhonen), 180—187(Markku Alatalo), 188, 189—191(Markku Alatalo), 192—193(Pietinen), 194(E. Holmén), 195—196(Jaerke Foto), 197, 198—200, 203—204(Ilmari Kostiainen), 205, 206(Ilmari Kostiainen), 207 (Max Petrelius), 208—218(Ilmari Kostiainen), 219—220(Max Petrelius), 221—223(Ilmari Kostiainen), 224(Saurén), 225—226(Ilmari Kostiainen), 227, 228—230(Ilmari Kostiainen), 231(Pietinen), 232(Kolmio), 233—239 (Ilmari Kostiainen), pages 12—13 and 145 (Ilmari Kostiainen).

Museum of Finnish Architecture   59, 60, 61(Simo Rista), 72, 73(G. Welin), 74, 83, 133(H. Havas), 244, 245(G. Welin), 249(Ingervo), 251(Kari Hakli), 252(Ingervo), 253(G. Welin), 254, 255(H. Havas), 256(Ingervo), 257—258(Simo Rista), 259(L. Mosso), 260, 261(Simo Rista), 262, 263(Simo Rista), 264(Kari Hakli), 265(Ingervo), 266(Simo Rista), 267(L. Mosso), 268—270, 271(H. Havas), 272(Heinonen), 273(Ingervo), 274, 275(E. Mäkinen), 276—277(H. Havas), 278—279(L. Mosso).

Nordiska Museet, Stockholm   87a.

Hakon Ahlberg: *Gunnar Asplund Arkitekt*. Stockholm 1943.   62.

Renato De Fusco: *Le Corbusier designer: i mobili del 1929*. Milano 1976.   66, 68.

W.R. Lethaby: *Philip Webb and His Work*. London 1935.   57, 58.

Göran Schildt: *Valkoinen pöytä: Alvar Aallon nuoruus ja taiteelliset perusideat*. Keuruu 1982.   63—65, 70, 71.

Christopher Wilk: *Marcel Breuer: Furniture and Interiors*. New York 1981.   67.

Aalto: Architecture and Furniture. The Museum of Modern Art, New York 1938.   107, 116.

Alvar Aalto vs. the Modern Movement. Published by the International Alvar Aalto Symposium, Jyväskylä 1981.   69.

Herbert Bayer: Das künstlerische Werk 1918—1938. Bauhaus-Archiv, Berlin 1982.   138.

[Wohnbedarf furniture catalogue].   89, 99.

Domus 1930/8—10.   98.

The following persons have been interviewed and consulted for information in Ms Parko's article: **179**

MARTTI ANTTILA, Interior Architect
Artek 1951—55

MAIRE GULLICHSEN, Professor
Artek, founder 1935—

SINIKKA KILLINEN, Textile Designer
Artek 1948—

PAAVO KORHONEN, Managing Director
Huonekalutehdas Korhonen Oy

PEKKA KORHONEN, Managing Director
Oy Pekka Korhonen Ltd.

JAAKKO KOSKINEN, Carpenter
Huonekalutehdas Korhonen Oy

HELLEVI OJANEN, Interior Architect
Artek 1947—52, 1956—58

KAARLO PAASIKIVI, Carpenter
Huonekalutehdas Korhonen Oy

MARJA PYSTYNEN, Textile Designer
Artek 1956—

SONJA SANDELL, M.A.
Artek 1940—79

BEN AF SCHULTÉN, Artistic Director, Interior Architect
Artek 1964—

ÅKE TJEDER, Managing Director, Consul General
Artek 1955—

PIRKKO VAARA-STENROS, Interior Architect
Artek 1956—61

AARNE VIRTA, Carpenter
Huonekalutehdas Korhonen Oy

RITTER LIBRARY
BALDWIN-WALLACE COLLEGE